NOTHING AS WE NEED IT

Before you start to read this book, take this moment to think about making a donation to punctum books, an independent non-profit press,

@ https://punctumbooks.com/support/

If you're reading the e-book, you can click on the image below to go directly to our donations site. Any amount, no matter the size, is appreciated and will help us to keep our ship of fools afloat. Contributions from dedicated readers will also help us to keep our commons open and to cultivate new work that can't find a welcoming port elsewhere. Our adventure is not possible without your support.

Vive la Open Access.

Fig. 1. Detail from Hieronymus Bosch, *Ship of Fools* (1490–1500)

NOTHING AS WE NEED IT: A CHIMERA. Copyright © 2022 by Daniela Cascella. This work carries a Creative Commons BY-NC-SA 4.0 International license, which means that you are free to copy and redistribute the material in any medium or format, and you may also remix, transform and build upon the material, as long as you clearly attribute the work to the authors (but not in a way that suggests the authors or punctum books endorses you and your work), you do not use this work for commercial gain in any form whatsoever, and that for any remixing and transformation, you distribute your rebuild under the same license. http://creativecommons.org/licenses/by-nc-sa/4.0/

First published in 2022 by Risking Education
an imprint of punctum books, Earth, Milky Way.
https://punctumbooks.com

ISBN-13: 978-1-68571-060-6 (print)
ISBN-13: 978-1-68571-061-3 (ePDF)

DOI: 10.53288/0382.1.00

LCCN: 2022940924
Library of Congress Cataloging Data is available from the Library of Congress

Book design: Vincent W.J. van Gerven Oei
Cover image: kevinmholmes, "Alchemy," *Flickr,* January 25, 2012.

spontaneous acts of scholarly combustion

Risking Education

Daniela Cascella
Nothing As We Need It

A Chimera

Acknowledgments

Nothing As We Need It rewrites and expands parts of my Ph.D. dissertation, *Nothing As We Need It: For Chimeric Writing*, fully funded by Sheffield Hallam University (2018–2021). Many thanks to my supervisors Sharon Kivland, Penny McCarthy, Alice Bell, to my examiners Zoë Skoulding and Hester Reeve, and to Becky Shaw, for supporting my research.

Thank you Susan Tomaselli, Julia Calver and Katarina Ranković, for inviting me to read from work in progress at the *Writing Is… Sound* event (Maynooth University) and at the *Writing for Practice Forum* (Goldsmiths University of London/Sheffield Hallam University); Jessica Sequeira, for publishing an earlier version of the "Impossible Interviews, Imaginary Conversations" section in *Firmament* #3 (Sublunary Editions); and James Hutchinson and Laura Haynes, for inviting me to talk about Chimeric Writing in the Art Writing MLitt at The Glasgow School of Art.

I am grateful as ever to Craig Dworkin, David Toop, Jennifer Hodgson, Kate Briggs, Tristan Foster, for their friendship, and for responding with encouragement to this project in its early stages; to Dominique Hurth, for asking me to write a text in her *Mixtape* where I first heard the song of Chimera; and to Colin, beyond words.

My immense gratitude to Ansgar and Emile, for welcoming this book into Risking Education with extraordinary insight, commitment, and enthusiasm.

This book would not exist without Yanina Spizzirri. It is dedicated to her, to Penny, and to Sharon.

Note

This book echoes, foreshadows, and interferes with its non-identical twin project *Chimeras: A Deranged Essay, An Imaginary Conversation, A Transcelation* (Sublunary Editions, 2022), which echoes, foreshadows, and interferes with this book.

Prelude: The Year Before

The Interdisciplinary Death of D.C.

I'm surrounded by disciplines.[1]

Disciplines!

So plural, so diverse…

Will they leave me in peace?

How imperious they appear together, these disciplines, and their interdisciplinarity,

[waltz]:
-arity, -arity, -arity,
-ity, -ity, -ity,
-ty, -ty, -ty,
-y, -y, -y,

how authoritative.

---

1 The beginning of this section echoes, and in part distorts Henri Michaux, "Fate: B," in *A Certain Plume,* trans. Richard Sieburth (New York: New York Review of Books, 2017), 131.

-y!

When all these disciplines approach me, it is with utmost brutality,

-ality! -ality!

Look at them:

Art, interested in voice;
Literature, desiring to listen;
and Sound Studies… Sound Studies wants to sing.

[thud]

[unbearable violent noises, of flesh being brutally torn]

[pause]

[voice from the other side]:

They ripped me apart in four,
ears, tongue, legs, hands.

I was drawn and quartered by the Interdisciplinary Nothing.

-Y!

It was a blood bath.

Voice from a Faintspeaker [deceptively luring the readers into an illusion of clarity, which shall be shattered in its reverberations]: Here rebegins *Nothing As We Need It,* in which a new and impure form of critical writing is imagined, enacted, and studied.[2] This form is named *chimeric* from the mythological Chimera — a fire-breathing monstrous creature made of three different parts, impossible in theory but real in the imagination, and in the reading of the myth. Similarly this book is a composite of interrelated parts written in different styles, some of which may seem impossible, monstrous, disturbing. It demands and proposes neologisms, a new vocabulary, and wildly imaginative approaches to reading and to writing criticism. Recursive and polyphonic, it questions linear ways of presenting scholarship in words and writes possibilities for citation beyond the limits of inverted commas. It argues for, and at once manifests, critical writing as enmeshment and conversation with its subject matters.

A chimera is also the object of a yearning deemed unattainable: this book exists in the space of such yearning, in the tension between words and that which exceeds them. The critic who writes is exhausted by such yearning, rather than the owner of exhaustive knowledge; scholarship and knowledge are chimeric — composite, monstrous, longing.

Instead of writing monographic studies as a distant critic, a three-voiced character speaks with the subjects of her study, inhabits their words, yearns to become them, and shows what composite and impure forms critical writing may take when words seem to be missing; how to transmit material that is untranslated, barely audible, or so close that it smothers; what types of bilingualisms, beyond the literal, are at play, for example writing criticism when the substance of study eludes words because it is made primarily of haunting voices, or tones.

---

2   To rebegin comes from Laura (Riding) Jackson's *The Telling*. It marks the sense of repetition in research, the way in which the beginning of every project is never a tabula rasa but emerges from, and contains residues of, the past. Laura (Riding) Jackson, "The Idea of Rebeginnings," in *The Telling,* ed. Michael Schmidt (Manchester: Carcanet, 2005), 85–107.

The many-voiced author of this book writes in English as a second language. She is a stranger. No matter how fluent, she is never entirely in synch with words that are hers not all hers, a small variance is always perceived. Writing as a stranger entails the perception of both loss and haunting: the loss of references when working with Italian writers not translated in English, and how these writers haunt the text even if they cannot be quoted. Chimeric writing takes shape beyond and before translation, attempts writing when there seem to be no words, not only across languages but across different mediums, in a confusion, re-telling, and distortion of sources.

Nothing As We Need It embraces exaggeration, laughter, and self-parody as legitimate forms in the writing of research. It makes a case for modes of address often deemed to be nothing in the conventions of scholarly writing and demonstrates that writing *nothing* as criticism does not mean this form of criticism is useless. *We need it,* the title states. Such a need demands composite, monstrous, fire-breathing manners of writing, and reading; introduces aural multiplicities, intermissions, and conversations; reveals that the apparent nothing is in fact full of signals which call for different ways of tuning into, and writing, the material of study.

How to read this? All through, to apprehend its volumes and echoes. With your ears. Listening to literature beyond the limits of textual analysis, the book asks to dismiss the visual implications of the term *reflection,* which assumes detachment and polished surfaces, in favor of an aural method of *resonance,* which allows enmeshment and interference. It expands on a non-exclusively Anglophone tradition of transformative critical work that unsettles language, welcomes imaginative wordplay, and shifts critical writing's tendency to cite from pre-validated sources into a sonorous practice of *csiting* where to cite is to site, to find and found grounds for writing by listening to one's references, no matter how obscure, and to arrange them in assonant encounters.

As a chimera, this book prompts multiple readings and shows composite and impure ways of transmitting knowledge and of learning while listening to texts in conversation. Knowing, in these pages, is related to *gnosis,* not to *episteme.* It is shaped through encounters with, and awareness of the metaphysical realities of a reading-writing-listening-composite self as it hears and speaks with others rather than through discursive arguments laid out in progression. Examples, motives, and contexts are given and commented throughout, always sounding like an introduction until the very last page, always an ending, always a beginning. The book continues to say what it is doing, to remark on its doing it, to rebuild its language. Sometimes it sounds as if it has been heard before. Sometimes it sounds like nothing, as we need it.

The three voices are haunted, unsettled, challenged, prompted, comforted, interrupted, inspired, exhilarated, exasperated, and exhausted by the subjects of their study, and this book enfolds such a range of states. The voices rehearse forms derived from dreams of criticism, which, in commenting on the works of other writers, comment at once on their own, embodying a yearning for them and a sense of kinship not without its conflicts. Chimeric writing is characterized by such kinship, conflict, and yearning toward its subjects, as much as by wordplay and self-parody adopted as devices of otherness. The voices are not tied by plot but move throughout the text as echoes of one another, in different tones. At times they blur into one another, signifying the oscillations in a writing self who is one and many. There is no concern with continuity or plausibility. There may be contradictions in the unravelling of the text, emphasizing the time loops, returns, premonitions, and residual strains that occur in research, as well as the sense of artificiality and strangeness at the heart of this study. Sometimes they interrupt and contradict one another. They are together, and never in synch.

D.C., between wit and gravitas, exhausted by literature, is dead, and always rebeginning as *Da Capo.* She has the habit of using *we* to signify her many voices. This is by no means intended to make generic assumptions on her readership. She is also known, much to her chagrin, as "that Italian who writes about sound"; has a tendency to fall, in the words of other writers; in a faint, like many of the enchanted lovers in the Arabian Nights; in faint signals. She learned the effects of repetition by listening to The Swans: when it seems enough, one more round will keep the listener enthralled, though slightly uneasy in the sweet torture of refrain. One more. Swan, from the Indo-European root *swen-, is to sound.[3] It is oddly assonant with the Italian *svanire,* to disappear. Writing for D.C. is at once to sound, and to vanish.

Cristina Rovina patiently collects and comments on D.C.'s unfinished texts. Cristina comes from the Italian writer Cristina Campo, who used at least four pseudonyms and whose words haunted D.C. in her lifetime.[4] *Rovina* is the Italian for ruin, a nod at the sense of writing-as-ruin that pervades these pages. The rhyme heard in Cristina Rovina is a response to the irritating rhyme that Italians will hear in the frequent misspelling made by Anglophones when they write *Daniella Cascella,* instead of Daniela Cascella. In Italian the pronunciation of Daniella is drastically different from the pronunciation of Daniela: it makes the first name rhyme with the surname.[5] It sounds like a

---

3 *Online Etymology Dictionary,* s.v. "*swen," https://www.etymonline.com/word/*swen-.
4 Cristina Campo's (1923–77) work is barely translated in English. A poet, essayist, and translator, she "wrote little, and wished she'd written less" but in fact published a lot, in pseudonyms, and in letters to friends which are considered among the best examples of epistolary writing in Italian literature. Her writings are at the core of Cascella's PhD research at Sheffield Hallam University (2018–21). A comprehensive biography in Italian is Cristina De Stefano, *Belinda e il mostro: Vita segreta di Cristina Campo* (Milan: Adelphi, 2002). See also Andrea di Serego Alighieri and Nicola Masciandaro, eds., *Glossator Journal* 11: "Cristina Campo: Translation / Commentary" (2021).
5 From the memoirs of German poet Heinrich Heine, reported by Daniel Heller-Roazen, *Echolalias: On the Forgetting of Language* (New York: Zone Books, 2005), 35: "Here in France my German name, 'Heinrich,' was translated into 'Henri' […]. I had to resign myself to it and finally name myself thus in this country, for the word 'Heinrich' did not appeal to the French ear […]. They were also incapable of pronouncing the name 'Henri Heine' correctly, and for most people my name is Mr. Enri Enn; many abbreviate this to 'Enrienne', and some called me Mr. Un Rien." From "Henrich

joke. And like a joke, one might say that in her youth Cristina "The Astonishing" Rovina became familiar with five foreign languages, the *Corpus Hermeticum,* calculus, ancient legends, sacred verses and the reasons for their revelation, philosophy, and rhetoric. She is fond of music and can play the theremin. A joke, exactly. Let us posit, however, the importance of contemplating the impossible in a character that is a chimera.

Impossible like The Ruin of Casc, or The Voice from a Faintspeaker. Invisible to the preoccupied gaze of reason, she can be heard sparsely but incisively in italics, or between brackets, or as phantom frequency. Assonant with the title of Roberto Calasso's book *The Ruin of Kasch* (in Italian, *Casc* and *Kasch* are pronounced exactly the same), R.C. is never entirely there, and haunts the text like a benign version of Maldoror, if such an entity may be envisaged. Never properly introduced — she has been addressing you, without much ceremony, since you started reading these pages — she is the incoherence in theory that makes perfect sense in practice, chimerically. It was suggested that The Ruin of Casc is the subtle noise of D.C.'s prose, or its tone, the silence that the writer imposes on her speech.[6]

Two other voices are heard. Chimera, constantly pointing at its excess, aims to spark, monstrous and difficult as it is, not to seduce with smooth prose. Do not call Chimera interdisciplinary, or she will spit fire at you. Chimera draws immense pleasure in contradicting and interrupting Literature, a murmur once heard in the singularity of an encounter. It is, with Ingeborg Bachmann, the elusive substance that continues to prompt writ-

---

Heine" to "a nothing." Further notes on the poetic potential of names and their sounds are in Craig Dworkin, "The Onomastic Imagination," in *Radium of the Word: A Poetics of Materiality* (Chicago: University of Chicago Press, 2020), 48–78.

[6] "Tone is not the voice of the writer, but the intimacy of the silence he imposes on his speech, which makes this silence still his own, what remains of himself in the discretion that sets him to one side." Maurice Blanchot, "The Essential Solitude," in *The Gaze of Orpheus and Other Literary Essays,* ed. P. Adams Sitney, trans. Lydia Davis (New York: Station Hill, 1981), 70.

ing.[7] It "grows," with Calasso, "like grass between the heavy gray paving stones of thought."[8]

They all sound as if speaking from The Other Side, or after fainting.

---

[7] Ingeborg Bachmann, *Letteratura come utopia,* trans. Vanda Perretta (Milan: Adelphi, 1993), 119–24.

[8] Roberto Calasso, *Literature and the Gods,* trans. Tim Parks (London: Vintage, 2001), 183.

Imaginary Conversation

Chimera and Literature

Dark and the night is clear, and D.C. is dead, her quartered body lying on the ground. From the sky, or from the depths of the earth, two monstrous beings appear whose nature does not look human. They nonetheless seem natural, as always in the logic of the Vision.[1] *The two creatures are*

> *Chimera, The Unnameable*
> *and*
> *Literature, The Timeless.*

They sit at either side of D.C.'s body and begin to speak.

One might say the two creatures speak to each other in verses, or in music. Granted, the effect and distortion of the vision allows them to sound like that; otherwise, their conversation may sound deprived of mystery, like an exchange of opinions, a dry report or commentary on the words of D.C., forever anguished by Literature and by her chimeric yearning for who knows what

---

[1] This scenario echoes Lucian of Samosata, "The Vision: A Chapter of Autobiography," in *The Works of Lucian of Samosata*, trans. H.W. Fowler and F.G. Fowler (Charleston: Forgotten Books, 2007), 20–23, echoed in turn in Pier Paolo Pasolini, "Note 3: Introduction of the Metaphysical Theme," in *Petrolio*, trans. Ann Goldstein (London: Secker and Warburg, 1997), 6–9.

sort of writing. In those words, however, coming from others, the writing of D.C. finds some sense, from another time, from the outer edges of a buried age. In truth, neither was her voice ever whole, even, or balanced, nor were her senses, certainly not her writing — and how could they be whole, even, and balanced, if she was so many voices, always more than one, groundless but not without grounds, her not all her?

Chimera, The Unnameable, who likes to laugh: Look at this D.C., poor wretch, quartered by the Interdisciplinary Nothing. A mystery I can recognize.

Literature, The Timeless, who exudes solemnity: It appears she has nothing to say.

C.: Her voice not all hers, surely she is mine.

L.: Yes, but the weight she carries inside, that belongs to me.[2]

C.: If this is the body of someone absorbed by writing as resonant space, and said she was writing criticism for the sake of the constellation of writers she read and derived her writing from; if she did not make her difficulties in a foreign language an excuse to stop writing, then this body is mine.

L.: Fair enough, but the weight she carries inside, that belongs to me.

C.: If D.C. maintained that her thoughts around chimeric writing were formed from the voices of other dead and unheard writers she frequented, then she belongs to me.

L.: [harsh, solemn, with obstinate persuasion, and the air of not giving up for any speculation in the world around the nature of

---

[2] Pasolini, "Note 3," 7.

critical writing]: Yes, but the weight she holds inside belongs to me.

C.: If this disconsolate D.C. did not aim to hold the words and voices of other writers for the sake of ventriloquism, or channeling, but to reinstate and situate herself as reader, then she is mine, speechless as she might feel.

L.: But the weight she carries inside is mine.

C.: D.C. was attempting to write around you, Literature, when you are not translated, or barely available. As if she could find any readers. She even asked others to join her, to no avail. Most withdrew, shied away at the invitation, concerned that the invisibility of materials would make writing invisible, too. The fools. That was the moment D.C. understood Gertrude Stein when she stated, "I write for myself and strangers," from a cusp of hope and despair.[3]

L.: Gertrude, how chimeric. How piercing, that moment when D.C. read, "You write a book and while you write it you are ashamed for every one must think you are a silly or a crazy one and yet you write it and you are ashamed, you know you will be laughed at or pitied by every one and you have a queer feeling and you are not very certain and you go on writing. Then someone says yes to it, to something you are liking, or doing or making and then never again can you have completely such a feeling of being afraid and ashamed that you had then when you were liking the thing and not any one had said yes about the thing."[4] Writing for oneself is not enough. You must have a chimeric yearning for someone who says, *yes*.

---

[3] Gertrude Stein, *The Making of Americans* (Champaign: Dalkey Archive Press, 1995), 289.
[4] Ibid., 485.

C.: …and D.C. went on writing. Persisting in her search to ground her words when the sources are opaque D.C. lost her voice and became many voices — like Pellegrina Leoni, the singer in Isak Dinesen's tale *The Dreamers,* who lost her voice and became many people.[5] Isak, another one with a pseudonym, "the one who laughs."[6]

L.: All good and right, laugh D.C. may. But the weight she carries inside is mine.

At this point Chimera sits down, looks into the distance: the distance of her yearning to take Literature away from herself. She realizes that she will never persuade Literature to laugh with her; and that solemn Literature's hammering repetitions, like a form of unholy rosary, beating, beating like a drum in the space of her thinking, are gradually beginning to possess her mind.

C.: What it is you wish to do, then?

L.: [who in truth is not averse to Chimera's inclinations but needs more time, Literature always needs more time]: My wish is to tell you what I taught D.C.; what she read in me before she came up with this most peculiar idea of bringing your bewitching laughter inside my world. I taught her that when there is apparently nothing to refer to, a different writing begins. Look at what Elfriede Jelinek did in her play *Her Not All Her,* which she wrote using the words of Robert Walser as material.[7] If these are not quoted directly, if page numbers are not given, but it is acknowledged that the text is shaped from them, then writing and reading become a question of resonance, presence, transformation.

---

5 Isak Dinesen [Karen Blixen], "The Dreamers," in *Seven Gothic Tales* (London: Penguin Books, 2002), 236–309.

6 Judith Thurman, *Isak Dinesen: The Life of Karen Blixen* (London: Penguin Books 1986), 23.

7 Elfriede Jelinek, *Her Not All Her: On/With Robert Walser,* trans. Damion Searls (London: Sylph Editions, 2012).

C.: What happens to the author?

L.: She is no longer a sole owner or creator of text. She exists in a mesh, not in a dictionary entry. She proceeds by a poetics of reminiscence, adding her singular voice, haunted by the other voices. You must understand, she never dissolves: she is her, not all her. This is not fragmentation: it is a process of individuation in which D.C. finds herself, having gone through a metamorphosis, enmeshed in the work of others, her voice at once faint, significant, and signifying. The poet Alejandra Pizarnik wrote, "I cannot speak with my voice, but I speak with my voices": she did not say *just voices* or *other voices*.[8] This is crucial: *it is me, Pizarnik and D.C. say, and I have many voices*. To further clarify, the use of many voices through pseudonyms adopted here is not like Søren Kierkegaard's, who firmly believed each of his pen names corresponded to a different philosophy. It is a way of being with, of being one and many, a way of presenting selfhood as enmeshment. Such multitude is the work of dedication, of recurrent reading.

C.: And the readers?

L.: The readers — implied, unborn, dead, or deaf — must be courageous, willing to move with and inside these words, and respond in turn, not to wait to be told everything. Do they trust the text? They can trust the telling in the text, the hum that keeps words together and demands a new way of reading that listens to the page. No safety net, other than the drive of the telling.

C.: *The Telling* is the title of a book by someone who dwelled in my realm for some time, Laura (Riding) Jackson, with her resolute, chimeric insistence on her writing being lodged in the

---

8   Alejandra Pizarnik, "Cornerstone," in *Extracting the Stone of Madness: Poems 1962–1972*, trans. Yvette Siegert (New York: New Directions, 2016), 97.

"durable sense of the further."[9] She spent many days conversing with me, telling me that "until the missing story of ourselves is told, nothing besides told can suffice us: we shall go on quietly craving it."[10] Words, and something missing — a chimeric yearning. She also told me that what we have to say "must be spoken with weighted reverberance, to be heard."[11] This reminds me of something D.C. wrote, on the need for faint signals to stay as such in order to be heard; not demanding loudness, but attention. The writer becomes a *faintspeaker*, inverts the loudspeaker's principle of amplification from loudness into a deepening. Laura also said something about "a book of one continual making."[12] This is also what Calasso wrote of you, Literature, as a quality which cannot be recognized by its "observance of any theory, but rather by a certain vibration or luminescence of the sentence" that connects books across the ages.[13] Writers are possessed by language, and you, Literature, speak along with them. Like Borges…

L.: May he rest in peace — you interrupted me. I was trying to say that in the case of Jelinek's play, because it is impossible to rely on the authority of footnotes, the reader is led deeply inside the text, as site of knowing in the experience of reading; and at once, the reader is taken outside the text, to inject some vitality again into the footnotes of her understanding, searching herself for Walser's books, finding her ways of reading them, wondering what echoes may be heard there. Jelinek's text does not rely on the scaffolding of references: it is all reference, or even better said, it is resonance. Its form does not need external systems of legitimization but is held together by the inner motor of understanding-through-reading.

---

9   Laura (Riding) Jackson, *The Telling*, ed. Michael Schmidt (Manchester: Carcanet, 2005), xv.
10 Ibid., 9.
11 Ibid., 43.
12 Ibid., 53.
13 Roberto Calasso, *Literature and the Gods*, trans. Tim Parks (London: Vintage, 2001), 175.

C.: I am beginning to follow you, Literature. I am beginning to see in which manners D.C. invoked me, before her fall.

L.: Jelinek was haunted by the words of Walser to the point of no longer knowing what is her and what not her —

C. [in a trance]: — "all and nothing."

L.: Calasso's argument around literature as a phosphorescent undercurrent that conjoins books became the thread that held together his publishing project Adelphi, and all his texts since the very first one, *The Mad Impure*.[14] The pages that D.C. wrote are themselves mad impurities in their ceaseless, stubborn, euphoric contaminations with the words of those who came before her.

C.: A monstrous task.

L.: Didn't someone once say that the sleep of reason generates monsters?[15]

C.: Chimeras. Didn't someone else once state that if humans lived their lives only based on reason, they would commit suicide?[16] That the horizon of imagination, of the possible, keeps people alive instead?

---

14 Roberto Calasso has been involved since 1962 in various editorial capacities, with the Italian publishing house Adelphi, responsible for translating in Italian a range of books by Mitteleuropean writers such as Alfred Kubin, Gottfried Benn, Ingeborg Bachmann, Thomas Bernhard, as well as works of mythology and religious studies, along with undertaking the publication of Friedrich Nietzsche's oeuvre. See Daniela Cascella, "The Secret Euphoria of Reading: On 'Cento lettere a uno sconosciuto' by Roberto Calasso," *3:AM Magazine*, November 24, 2015, https://www.3ammagazine.com/3am/the-secret-euphoria-of-reading-on-cento-lettere-a-uno-sconosciuto-by-roberto-calasso/.
15 Francisco Goya, "The Sleep of Reason Produces Monsters," aquatint, 1797–99.
16 Giacomo Leopardi, *Zibaldone di pensieri* (Milan: Feltrinelli, 2019), 275.

L.: Didn't you notice, D.C.'s initials signal a *Da Capo*?

C.: *Da Capo,* to rebegin, to write from the residues of what was before. After D.C. heard herself echoed, and as echo, in the words of other writers before she had read them, it seems a natural step for her to ask, who is the critic, who is the subject? She confused any hierarchy between the two, allowed the subjects of her research to speak about her, to speak with her.

L.: You know what happens to *voice* in her project, then.

C.: It becomes many voices. Bypassing estates, archives, permissions, working with *I heard* rather than *I document*; with the ambiguous authority of the storyteller rather than the sanctioned power of the document, words and voices imagine what is not there, and bring myself, chimera, into being; yearning for knowing, rather than filing knowledge under glass. Let's say there is an urgency.

L.: Then you want to write. So many who frequented me had to live with that most dreary of illnesses, the writer's block. But those who truly want to inhabit me, in front of the urgency of a telling, could not allow themselves to be stuck like Sisyphus. They adopted instead the transformation into the rock as method, they became their material. "How is it possible to know what does not allow itself to be known?" someone once asked, and replied, "only one way: becoming somehow that thing."[17] Questions in me are not to be answered but incite metamorphosis along their lines, for the sake of their cadence. "These pages become a place for me to inhabit their words and be haunted by them, sometimes transforming them into my reasoning, sometimes by imitation or echo alone, if they alone are possible."[18]

---

[17] Roberto Calasso, *L'ardore* (Milan: Adelphi, 2016), 57. Translations from Calasso's books are Rovina's, unless stated otherwise.
[18] Robert Duncan, *The H.D. Book,* eds. Michael Boughn and Victor Coleman (Berkeley: University of California Press, 2011), 404.

Searching for words, D.C. wrote her pages as vessels for a transformation, to work with their substance; becoming volume, sometimes transforming them into her reasoning, sometimes by imitation or echo alone.

C.: A critical study?

L.: Chimeric, you are about to suggest —

C.: Chimeric. D.C. speculated around criticism as yearning. Consider the simple fact that many of the works she studied were not translated in English. As you know D.C. is not a translator, so she had to adopt another mode to write. By now, you will have guessed how.

L.: Talking with the pages she read. For them she became volume. She made space for them, amplified them, and wrote. D.C. kept in mind, through and through, the definition given by Maurice Blanchot of critical discourse as the "space of resonance within which the unspoken, indefinite reality of the work is momentarily transformed and circumscribed into words."[19] This definition highlights the cohabitation of, and tension between words and excess of words at the core of D.C.'s work. It allowed her to practice and consider critical writing in a realm of resonance, imagination, and transmission, rehearsing a variety of forms and tones which allowed it to be called chimeric. Blanchot's "momentarily circumscribed" invites to think of critical writing as a vessel that holds a material which may at times be absent. Chimeric writing shows how such vessels may be formed, how their singular shapes are crucial in offering a sense of the tone of the elusive material they momentarily hold. Never forgetting the unspoken.

---

19 Maurice Blanchot, "Preface: What is The Purpose of Criticism?" in *Lautréamont and Sade*, trans. Stuart Kendall and Michelle Kendall (Stanford: Stanford University Press, 2004), 4.

C.: Reading and writing across two languages (and a dialect) belongs in a language larger than her own, in which kinships are awoken through difference — into which the cultural fabric of a self may be transposed. You might not read and perceive D.C.'s Italian materials as she does, but her yearning for them in English, circling around their impossible sense, generates a tension which is not meant to voice a private understanding. It is a tension toward an ungraspable something (toward me, Chimera) which makes her write in order to tell, to begin a conversation, away from any sheltered claims of integrity. D.C. attempted to shift the attention on writing as transmission of knowledge, changeable and impure, rather than on considerations of purity and fixity. She wanted to prove that when something cannot be quoted — be it the sound of a voice, be it a pigment, a frequency, a mood, the hum of untranslated literature — or cannot be read and heard in another language, it does not mean it does not exist. It can prompt conversations. I am chimera, D.C. is chimeric, her writing not severed from the objects of its desire and yearning. There is no critical distance but stickiness of relation; wanting-to-become; utopias of critical writing as uninterrupted glossing, saying what is not there.

L.: What is not there and prompts to speak… Do you remember, "I have nothing to say and I am saying it and that is poetry as I need it"?[20] One day D.C. rewrote it as "we have nothing to say and we are saying it and that is criticism as we need it." Rewriting Cage, replacing *poetry* with *criticism,* and *I* with *we,* she enacted the writing of inhabitation that is one of the main aspects of her work. *We* sounds a polyphony: critical writing is enmeshed in conversations, at times silent or interior, haunting. D.C. may not have heard her voice when she spoke in English but heard many voices in writing, the voices of all the untranslated texts that shaped her language. So her work existed as Blanchot's resonant space, that allows various frequencies to cohabit.

---

20 John Cage, "Lecture on Nothing," in *Silence: Lectures and Writings* (New York: Marion Boyars, 2009), 109.

C.: Rewriting Cage, inhabiting his words with small variance, also opened possibilities for D.C. to write when there seemed to be nothing to say. Often she found herself speechless, not for want of thoughts or responses but not aligned with the forms such thoughts or responses were expected to take. Sometimes the lack of words ensued from her tendency to linger in the moment of the aesthetic encounter; sometimes it was due to that nuanced loss, that slight delay —

L.: — a slight delight —

C.: — that slight delay in finding the right words, experienced when writing in a second language. Other times it was the result of a feeling of displacement when looking for words while listening to their sounds. Always out of synch, always something missing. Writing when there is nothing to quote, words must do something else, embody a *mise-en-abyme* which at times becomes vertiginous, at times monstrous.

L.: Yet in the eye of the vertigo, D.C. found her words, monstrous and enmeshed. Individuation is not individualization; it is the gaining of a selfhood which is always in loss, never entirely full, structurally incapable of completion, and at once tending to it. All and nothing.

C.: Move your thoughts from nothing to say to *Empty Words,* the title of that piece performed by Cage in 1977 at Teatro Lirico in Milan, *his meticulous and monotonous dissection of Thoreau's diaries that began by omitting phrases, then words, then syllables until there was nothing but sounds. The atmosphere arose into an explosion of voices and dissent. There was Cage, his words weighing as much as the explosion of noises around. The audience started laughing, shouting, mocking, whistling, and booing till it all turned into a carnival of infuriating chaos. Cage? He kept reading, responding with poised rhythm to the tension around* […].

The explosion of voices from a hidden past clashed with an inner silence, with Cage's present tense.[21]

L.: Pre-sentence, I heard this before. Da Capo.

C.: Da Capo, D.C., Drawing on Cage as method, encaged in empty words as cadence and with it, persistence. No matter what, continue to attend to your task.

L.: And silence?

C.: The silence D.C. writes with is not an act of violence, or censorship, resulting in trauma. It is necessary, it is substance, it is medium. It is the resonant silence of —

L.: — of reading. Sometimes D.C. became silent when encountering works which manifested a deep secret. Suddenly it is there yet cannot be pronounced. Something profound is at play, in these lines of escape, these apparent *lacunae* — the discovery that something exists, the excitement of being there, and not disclosing that space entirely. Remember that astonishing page in Robert de Boron's thirteenth-century account of the Cycle of the Holy Grail, describing Joseph's vision in which he ate a whole heart, the intellect exceeding its formal limits, and yet returning to words to lead you toward somewhere; not to get there, but to lead you *toward*.[22] This is chimeric writing. All the states which brought a writer into being and are never entirely told, never entirely held. They transform the way in which a writer exists, day after day, and no record will ever hold them.

C.: The question of the ineffable as such did not concern D.C. *That* is beyond words. She was drawn to the tension between

---

21 Daniela Cascella, *En Abîme: Listening, Reading, Writing: An Archival Fiction* (Winchester: Zero Books, 2012), 37.
22 Robert de Boron, "La visione," trans. Cristina Campo, in *I mistici dell'Occidente*, ed. Elémire Zolla (Milan: Adelphi, 2010), 1:770.

what is written and what exceeds it and puts pressure on it, what forms it provokes. Vladimir Jankélévitch, writing about music and the ineffable, wonders if "the Charm" in music, the impossible-to-articulate that attracts, is "a form of deception or a principle of wisdom."[23] He wrote of "the thickness of […] meaning" where depth holds at once presence, a form of thick secrecy, and a ceaseless chimeric yearning for words.[24] Studying the ways in which the ineffable is made present in writing, D.C. encountered Michel de Certeau's *The Mystic Fable* in which the scholar shows that, no matter how *beyond words* the mystical experience might be, the fact that mystic texts exist, and they take the forms they take, cannot be denied. There begins a complex research into the various currents and undercurrents that move *across* texts —

L.: — the subtle noise of prose —

C.: — where chimeric writing exists as subtle noise, its presence shaping and being shaped by the silence that it holds, and that holds her murmuring quietude. It is there and must be acknowledged, even when it does not imply complete transparency, or accessibility. But — what are you holding in your hands now, Lit? Why the terror in your eyes?

Literature reads out loud an excerpt from THE PLAN FOR A BOOK *by D.C., from which may be gathered whether or not she was justly entitled to write in her lifetime.*

L.: "… a book entitled *Nothing As We Need It*, where a new form of critical writing is imagined, studied, and [PARTS DELETED] […] questions linear models of presenting scholarship in words. It argues for, and once manifests critical writing as enmeshment and conversation with its subject matters. At the core are two in-

---

23 Vladimir Jankélévitch, *Music and the Ineffable*, trans. Carolyn Abbate (Princeton: Princeton University Press, 2003), xxii.
24 Ibid., 70.

terrelated questions. How non-normative, and formally experimental, can scholarly writing be? How is it possible to articulate and transmit research in writing, and the writing of research, in ways that favor impurity over detachment; that are entangled rather than linear; that embrace exaggeration, repetition, laughter and self-parody as legitimate forms? The book will be a study of tones and forms, a commentary on its own process, the unravelling of philosophical concerns, and a manifestation of a writing meth — "

C. [interrupts, exasperated]: Enough! I've heard it before and cannot hear it anymore. I beg you Lit, give me some space to breathe. I did not realize D.C. would use my name so extensively. Look at me, Lit, I am a fire-breathing monster.

L.: Of course, you are lit, in part you are me. Who knows how many times, on your lowest harmonics, you sing with me? You are also the subject of an unattainable yearning. Curious, that D.C. employed the adjective *chimeric* —

C. [pleased with herself]: — how elegant.

L.: — to articulate her understanding of critical writing keeping these two qualities in mind: the monstrous, the unattainable. This form of writing — not entirely criticism, not entirely fiction, not entirely art, not entirely essay, them not all them — was displaced and replaced in the space of yearning, in the excess that prompted and grounded it.

C. [now exceedingly pleased with herself]: You will appreciate the shift in terminology proposed by D.C., from a functional designation such as *interdisciplinary* to *chimeric* —

L.: — from institutional rhetoric toward the realm of symbolic reading, allowing the term that defines her study to make its context, and the echoes that resound therein, present.

C.: Certainly to call me into play, to spell my composite being, brings about a sense of monstrosity, artifice, and mythical density in writing, along with associations and analogies that fall flat, and have no resonance with the term *interdisciplinary*. To say *chimeric* sets a mood, and a mode. It is not interchangeable, or arbitrary, but necessary: the term that holds the way in which writing is formed *is* the way of knowing it brings forth, and it shapes knowing. D.C. did not want to explain me, Chimera: she wanted to show what Chimera might engender in the imagination, prompting thought toward myth, toward monster, toward yearning.

L.: The form.

C.: Composite, monstrous, yearning.

L.: The composite, monstrous, yearning form by which writing is made and understood corresponds to the —

C.: — composite, monstrous, yearning —

L.: — form of the writer's being. You cannot detach the form in which a project is transmitted from its writer's metaphysical groundings, and the way they are in the world. Henry Corbin —

C.: — that excellent scholar of Islamic philosophy and Sufism who often talked to me.

L.: Corbin demonstrates this, when in his study of Avicenna he states, "[e]ach of us carries in himself the Image of his own world, his *Imago mundi* […]. [This] offers us not only philosophemes to be studiously learned, but symbols […], their universe is neither dead, nor outpassed, nor transcended. For in the measure to which an author rises to symbols, he cannot himself exhaust the significance of his work. This significance remains latent in the pleroma of symbols."[25] Symbols, the forms in which a project is articulated, do not "submit to the data" but "propose tasks — even if their effort is not to bear fruit until after they are laid in the grave."[26] As a *situative* practice of writing, and of thinking, chimeric writing is never exhaustive, and never *situated* in given frameworks, but it orients itself as an operation steeped in desire that establishes its singular ontology, constellations of references, and shapes.[27] These may, at times, seem nothing.

C.: *Nothing* also means nothing obvious, or immediate. What else can be heard, D.C. asked, if given terms are dismissed in the writing of research, and lower or less expected frequencies are broadcast? What does this attuned hearing, this hearing of nothing, bring about, in its core?

L.: The core, *situative*… I hear again echoes of Corbin, whose insights into learning as "opening our possibilities to ourselves" instead of accumulating "vain erudition," finding oneself always as Stranger, always singular in one's mode of perceiving and comprehending, which corresponds to one's mode of being, stirred many thoughts in her, before her fall.[28]

C.: You are acute. Remember how D.C. became more and more drawn to Corbin's idea that the mode of presence is what determines the quality of how we learn and think and know. *How*: not form as an empty shell but form as the necessary and inevitable articulation that could not be otherwise, because it is tied to being.

---

25 Henry Corbin, *Avicenna and the Visionary Recital*, trans. Willard R. Trask (Princeton: Princeton University Press, 1988), 8–9.
26 Ibid., 11.
27 For an illustration of situative modes of presence, see Corbin, *Avicenna and the Visionary Recital*, and Tom Cheetham, *The World Turned Inside Out: Henry Corbin and Islamic Mysticism* (New Orleans: Spring Journal Books, 2015).
28 Ibid., 10.

L.: How are you, Chim?

C.: How do you perceive me, before thinking about it? What moves your language, before constraining it under systems and frames? So in every research project, in every supervision encounter, in every writing instance, instead of imposing existing and validated frames, the question becomes, can a constellation of references be assembled from the core that moves each project?

L.: *That* made D.C. exhausted. Instead of writing exhaustive monographs about her subjects as a distant critic, she spoke with them, exhausted as she may have been she inhabited their words, longed to be with them, yearned for them.

C.: This form of writing does not aim to reach the conclusion of argument but the presence of heartbeat, following on words that other writers inhabited before, and that could later be inhabited, writing along those lines, dispersing, detouring. There is no wholeness but consciousness breaking through dismemberment. Here D.C. encounters Blanchot's words at the end of *The Song of the Sirens,* calling for "the infinite movement which is the encounter itself" and reinstates its own, imaginal time.[29]

L.: "Always still to come, always in the past already, always present."[30] Let's disappear now. Allow more of D.C.'s words to be read, heard.

---

29 Maurice Blanchot, "The Song of the Sirens," in *The Gaze of Orpheus and Other Literary Essays,* ed. P. Adams Sitney, trans. Lydia Davis (New York: Station Hill, 1981), 112.
30 Ibid.

The End of D.C.'s Last Lecture, Followed by a Disastrous Q&A

"What is knowing before knowledge? What is known in hearing, before it is thought to be known in reading? Writing nothing as we need it lifts words off the page, works with their excess. It relies on fine-tuning of senses and unveils the plenitude of listening; of conversations even when impossible, or imagined. Nothing as we need it is the plenitude of being plural. *Distracted by the coughs of exasperation and discomfort from the audience, who came here to hear a soothing monologue not a troubling lecture, D.C. begins to accelerate her reading, in a helpless state of infra-panic. At times her voice breaks.* You might recall Hélène Cixous, who states that when we begin to read, we understand nothing, we are blind and ignorant, and yet we know we are there.[1] I am curious about how it is possible to begin and articulate words *there,* what happens in this condition of apparent blindness, ignorance, and presence. I believe it allows to steer the attention toward less audible or visible elements. *There* is re-constituted, re-claimed, by *csiting* — not quoting from legitimized sources but from those sources that made us, no matter how abstruse and out of place they might be. (*Situative, not situ-*

---

1   Hélène Cixous, *Three Steps on the Ladder of Writing*, trans. Sarah Cornell and Susan Sellers (New York: Columbia University Press, 1993), 24.

ated.) Csiting conjoins *citing* and *siting*: to listen to one's references and arrange them in assonant desiring encounters. It is a way of working with texts beyond the rules of citation, a way of citing as hearing the voices of others in reading and recalling them in writing. The writer finds her grounds as she reads, sites herself as she cites, goes over the words that made her understanding of chimera. Sources are not origins, understood in terms of a *before* that legitimates and authorizes what is written. They are not frames; they are beating hearts, cores. I want to show what happens when we do not feel entirely stable or safe in our stride, and yet continue to read, and write. 'Groundless but not without grounds,'[2] someone once said."

Silence. No questions from the audience. D.C. softly hums the traditional American folk song I Wish I Was a Mole in the Ground, *described by music critic Greil Marcus as "almost impossible to comprehend […] a nothing, an impossible negation."*[3]

Chair [performing enthusiasm]: Thank you so much, D.C. Such an insightful reading!

D.C. [inner voice]: A sinkhole in the ground.

D.C.: Hm, yes, thank you, it was great to read here tonight.

D.C. [inner voice]: May a sinkhole in the ground open, now, swallow the entire building and all of us, spare us the farce of this conversation.

Chair [emphatically]: Your research is so interesting, now tell me something more about *voice,* about *sound,* and about *silence.*

---

2 Elfriede Jelinek, "Sidelined," Nobel Lecture, Swedish Academy, Stockholm, Sweden, December 7, 2004, https://www.nobelprize.org/prizes/literature/2004/jelinek/lecture/.

3 Greil Marcus, *Lipstick Traces: A Secret History of the Twentieth Century* (Cambridge: Harvard University Press, 1989), 16.

THE END OF D.C.'S LAST LECTURE

D.C. [inner voice]: Sure, and while you're at it, explain in five minutes, to a non-specialist audience, Gödel's theorems of incompleteness…

D.C.: I do not think this is a good starting point.

D.C. [inner voice, humming the song to herself]: "Drink your blood like wine."

Chair: And what did you mean to express in this monologue?

D.C. [now embodying the half-incredulous, half-mocking expression of Orson Welles in Pasolini's film *La Ricotta*]: My most intimate, profound, archaic conformism.[4]

Chair [conforming to her script, that is, not listening]: *Sound* and *voice* are so relevant in art discourses today, aren't they? Maybe you could start from *the non-alignment of sonic criticality*?

D.C. [inner voice, in waltz rhythm]: Ality, ality, ality… How can you ask me about a sensibility toward sound, when you have just programmed me to read in a hall with horrible acoustics, where it was barely possible for my voice to be heard? I need to disappear, now.

D.C.: I'm exhausted; I don't think I can do this.

D.C. faints, falls on the floor.

---

4   "La ricotta," on *Ro.Go.Pa.G.*, dir. Pier Paolo Pasolini (1962/63; Eureka Entertainment, 2012), DVD.

A Questionnaire (with a Not Too Hidden Agenda) for the Readers — Authors Unknown

How many times have you silenced obscure references in favor of more current ones, knowing that by doing so you stand a higher chance of being heard?

Do you always need a massive wall of loudspeakers behind you?

Even when your wall of sound is, in fact, a ruin?

In other words, when you are about to write criticism, do you choose to quote whomever you choose to quote because they are validated, current in certain discourses?

Do you realize that by doing so you silence those writers who operate in the same field but do not have the same means of amplification?

Do you realize you will burn in hell, for mentioning same old same old?

What can critical writing make manifest if detached from judgements of value?

What form of knowing emerges from being plurally attuned, not just one, not just self?

What takes shape and is heard in writing, when you say you have nothing to say?

Voice from a Faintspeaker: A Chimera?

Impossible Interviews, Imaginary Conversations

A Deranged Essay by Cristina Rovina, with Interferences by the Voice from a Faintspeaker

The book that exhausted D.C. was written by Giorgio Manganelli, its title *Le interviste impossibili* (*The Impossible Interviews*).[1] Not translated in English from Italian to date, the Adelphi edition contains twelve imaginary conversations between an elusive interviewer and dead characters across history and legend such as Marco Polo, Harun al-Rashid, Tutankhamun, evoked through ambiguous traits of their personality that suffuse the pages with the metaphysical light of their absurd premise.

Voice from a Faintspeaker: A book around critical writing that is a chimera, impossible.

Impossible the book's title, impossible for D.C. to write about it. It is an extraordinary book and she, exhausted, could not find words for its extra. Yet she knew she must never cease to seek, attempt, and find forms and ways of telling what seems impossible. Otherwise it would continue to stay invisible, inaudible.

---

1   Giorgio Manganelli, *Le interviste impossibili* (Milan: Adelphi, 1997).

VfaF: A work on reading as kinship, even when there seem to be no words, inaudible.

D.C. kept the book on her desk, in her bag, near her bed, took it with her on flights and train journeys, underlined its pages until the pencil marks cut through the paper — signs of bodily pressure into the impossible-to-tell, the pencil sharpened as if to compensate for the lack of a sharp point in her understanding. Perhaps no sharpness is necessary here, but a more unstable quality that lodges in hearing. What voices are heard in those impossible interviews? *Heard,* after all, is an anagram of *read* with the added h of a breath. Listening here lifts words off the page, into a realm of resonance. As I listen to those imaginary conversations I find myself entangled, in the undulating imprecision and presence of voices heard in reading, which demands a language equally present, undulating, impure.

VfaF: A study of new possibilities for citation, beyond the boundaries of inverted commas.

D.C. had nothing to write but the necessity of staying with the book, yearning for its words, and for writing nothing, and for more words, which may hold the time spent with it, all and nothing, she had nothing or at least she had nothing *forward,* conventionally. Nothing that could fulfil the common expectations of writing about a book as *reviewing,* offering context, analysis, judgement, to dissect it by means of erudition. But D.C. never read for erudition, she read for connections, even when most unlikely, or unhinged. Sometimes the hinges would break, and she was left with a silence so deafening that she could only fill it with laughter.

VfaF: It demands other ways of reading, which enfold hearing.

So she wrote, so I write, in enmeshment rather than distance, seeking resonance rather than reflection, connection rather than content, not reading as a distant critic, but hearing and engaging in a conversation with those characters, in agreement as much as interruption, interference, disturbance. She could not take the book as a case study, she shattered the glass case under which the material of study is kept and longed for a writing of weighted reverberance and enmeshment, inside and with. *Because* the conversation is impossible, and because she heard it in reading, she had to write it.

VfaF: A text made of words, and "something more and something else" than words?[2]

Writing with apparently nothing to say allowed D.C., her not all her, and myself to spend more time listening; it intimates a need to stay with, sustain, attend. The form of writing, the condition of writing, and the writer are made and manifested of the same substance. When this substance feels empty, words require a timeless pace, and the writer will be still. The emptiness of argumentation in front of a book manifests a vessel forming, modes of reaching the margin, the recursive nature of knowing, instead of the visibility and mass of knowledge. Such present-and-absent conversation happens in the form it happens, which says something about how we (D.C. and I) listen, how we fabricate language, the kinships we perceive, the sympathetic frequencies which draw us to certain materials, in singular acts of reading through tonal encounters, always akin, always slightly out of synch, and then again — exhaustion, excitement, the ways in which a critic grasps for that secret core, that mass of yearning, emotion, interference, incongruence, and thinking with her materials that make her write.

VfaF: Something more and something else than words.

---

2   "[E]ach word says what is says — and beyond that, something more and something else." Alejandra Pizarnik, "The Shapes of Absence: The Word that Heals," in *Extracting the Stone of Madness: Poems 1962–1972*, trans. Yvette Siegert (New York: New Directions, 2016), 117.

[C.R. begins to hear the *Voice from a Faintspeaker* humming in her head. Startled, but never averse to experimenting with abstruse ways of knowing and understanding, she attempts to reply, even if unsure if she is addressing a voice nested inside herself, the voice of D.C., or Literature proper.]

All this, and more. The chimera of the impossible interviews, of entertaining conversations with dead or semi-fictional characters, of summoning the departed, recalls a statement I once heard in Calasso's *The Ruin of Kasch*: the dead are, in fact, books. They dwell in pages, "solidified into portable objects that accompany us, prey on us, haunt us, assuage us."[3] In Manganelli's book of impossible interviews, D.C. heard a resonance proper of the book's material. Inert, those conversations with the dead are never entirely told, they cannot be quoted, they must first and foremost be imagined, chimerically. *Then* they might be heard.

VfaF: Heard, after all, is an anagram of read *with the added* h *of a breath. Here chimeric writing yearns to become it subjects. Hear chimeric writing.*

Manganelli's book is written in Italian. D.C. was not a translator, and what drives a critic who is exhausted from dwelling in the entanglements of reading, but is not exhaustive in mentioning sources she cannot quote? Exhausted, worn out, like the smoothed feet of those marble statues in Italian churches that have been touched so many times they have lost their initial form, only to carry the stamp of devotion that often is obsession, the erasing and changing mark of time spent, which may smoothen, which may smother. So the critic and her subjects are spent, worn out, transformed. To study means to change; not to attend to a fixed object, but to transform it and be transformed with it.

---

3   Roberto Calasso, *The Ruin of Kasch,* trans. Richard Dixon (London: Penguin Books, 2018), 353.

VfaF: Dismissing the "case study" model, this form of writing shatters the glass under which the material of research is kept, and becomes a writing inside *and* with: *it is the Eleusinian suffering through, pathos and passion, where the achievement is not in concrete outputs, but in finding oneself exactly where one started, understanding deeper the way in which one is there, the manners of being, the ways of perceiving, the sympathies which draw one to engage with certain materials.[4]*

The impossibility of writing around Manganelli's impossible interviews was also bound to D.C.'s awareness of the book's faint sound — faint for its subjects at times baffling, at times abrasive, full of histories and themes so specific, non-topical, or out of currency, that they might sound empty. Who will receive? Who will tune in? When you are pushed outside of certain legitimate circles of literary anything, that deem you to be literally nothing, who is there to hear? Is amplification necessary when certain signals demand to stay faint? What is perceived as emptiness of argument is in fact a vessel forming, to hold a transformation of the residual and recursive materials of knowing, instead of the evidence and mass of knowledge. Caught between the need to transmit faint sounds, and the high chances of not being received, she longed for a type of hearing attuned to detect other faint voices, so it may divert from the apparent void-silence that is only a superficial contrast to loudness.

VfaF: This sounds as if it has been heard before.

---

4   Based on the myth of Demeter and Persephone, the Eleusinian Mysteries in ancient Greece consisted of rituals out of which the participants would emerge with no fear of death, and to which the initiates were sworn in agreement that no details would be divulged. Both Calasso and Simone Weil returned several times to Eleusis in their writings. The key sources in the reading of the Mysteries presented in this book are in Calasso's *Il cacciatore celeste* (Milan: Adelphi, 2019), and Weil's *First and Last Notebooks*, trans. Richard Rees (Eugene: Wipf & Stock, 2015) and Weil's *Gravity and Grace*, trans. Emma Crawford and Mario von der Ruhr (New York: Routledge, 2002).

There is no such thing as void-silence, there are volumes which will never be loud enough because if they do, they get distorted and lose texture. Better to tune in the hearing, than force a faint signal to scream. These signals may appear isolated because of the non-immediacy of references or cultural contexts they hold. They need wildly imaginative forms of hearing and reading, and impure forms of writing, monstrous writing-as-attuning, attuned hearing-in-reading. Perceived differently, they are perceived as different. They need another form of attuning, and of handing over. D.C. called this writing-as-attuning and the reading it demands, chimeric.

VfaF: This sounds like nothing, as we need it.

This form of attunement can be frightening. *Frightening*, as William Carlos Williams said to the Italian writer Cristina Campo on reading her words on his poetry: "I do not think that any one on this earth would ever find me out among my writings as you have done, or would care to do so much for me. You have turned me inside out, stripped me bare and I am not even embarrassed but on the contrary welcome you as a lover and a friend. Nothing physical about it; it goes deeper than that, is why I say it frightens me — we do not in this world admit such intimacies, we have to hide them from each other but you have found me out, I am frightened by it."[5]

I want to write this sense of being frightened and compelled by words that find me out when I read, the silence that continues to overwhelm and exhaust, makes me present and strange, the fullness of hearing voices in books, even if impossible, or dead — where words haunt me, from times before me, they are suddenly saturated with meaning, only to withdraw again, and I talk with them, I am eloquently interrupted by them, and disturbed, I take leave from them, and I am there, as I was nearly

---

5 Monica Farnetti and Giovanna Fozzer, eds., *Per Cristina Campo* (Milan: All'insegna del pesce d'oro, 1998), 107.

there, I have always been there, and have never been. To write yearning, which gives voices their purpose, even if it is only dust, even if the signal is faint. In monstrous mutations never mute. It is difficult to write this, groundless but not without grounds, and yet writing is my vessel, writing is my limit, my voices, my chimera, impure-monstrous-loud-silence that never allows me to think "I have done."[6]

---

[6] Laura (Riding) Jackson, *The Telling*, ed. Michael Schmidt (Manchester: Carcanet, 2005), 49.

Faint Signals

Lost Notes by D.C.

The German artist Rolf Julius made works of small sounds, for the downward gaze. I remember seeing those tiny speakers in the huge hall of the Hamburger Bahnhof in Berlin, hearing those faint sounds in the vast space around them. Their substance was not revealed through amplification, but through detail and stillness. Not loudness, but attention.

An image comes to my mind: a photo of the little speaker, half-buried in dust, from Julius's installation *Music in a Corner* (1983).[1] The list of materials in the work's caption includes cement powder, loudspeaker, audio,

and corner.

If you are a small speaker and you are partially buried in dust, do not consider yourself only a small speaker. Feel the dust, dwell on the angularity of the corner. They are all materials of what you do, even if they are outside yourself though immediately close, so why exclude them. Dismiss sterile subjectivism, think not only of yourself as a speaker but as a speaker endusted,

---

1 Rolf Julius, *Small Music (Grau)*, eds. Bernd Schulz and Hans Gercke (Heidelberg: Kehrer Verlag, 1995), 77.

encornered. The corner will be a frail frame, the dust will blow away, will transport the work and its sounds elsewhere.

Music, in Julius's titles, is often *for*: for a ruin, for a frozen lake, for the eyes, for an island, for a long time. It is itself and leans toward elsewhere, it holds an inclination. Sometimes a sound is a stone. In *Stone (Alone)* (1993) a loudspeaker emits faint sounds from the top of a stone; a faint broadcast, a heavy grounding.[2]

On answering a demand that his drawings should be more modern, he replies with a statement of return and repetition, "Always the same garden, always the same segment."[3]

On answering the criticism that the sounds in one of his installations may be "not loud enough," he says: "Can you imagine how loud a lotos sings?"[4]

David Toop writes of primitive *ground instruments* that employ strings across resonant holes in the ground, marginal or spectral sound-producing devices barely heard, if at all: "[T]hese holes in the ground address a basic problem — how to make a small thing bigger — and by applying the principle of resonance they fashion an elegant solution whose imprint will gradually soften and crumble into an impression rather than a scar. We could learn something from that."[5]

I long for writing that leaves impressions, not scars. I imagine an endless edit of a book that transmits other books that are punctuations in something that exceeds them and puts pressure on them, in time, holding time, unstable as they are composite, interfered with, suspended.

---

2   Ibid., 191.
3   Ibid., 139.
4   Ibid., 147.
5   David Toop, "Gone to Earth," *David Toop: A Sinister Resonance*, September 29, 2017, https://davidtoopblog.com/2017/09/29/gone-to-earth/.

Oh!

say Literature and Chimera, and that one utterance makes up in enraptured delivery what it lacks in intellectual sparkle.

Literature: O O   O O O O O O Oh
          Why — this?
    O   Oh   O O Oh — Why trouble
                           yourself uselessly?[6]

Chimera: I never read for erudition but for connections, even when most unlikely, or unhinged.

L.: As shades, that is our privilege.

Chimera [mildly startled]: I don't know, I think I heard something about crisis.

L.: The imaginary conversations are ways of voicing the crisis of all-encompassing thought, ways of making voices heard in fractured states, present out of nothing.

C.: Imaginary, impossible conversations such as the *Dialogues of the Dead* by Lucian of Samosata, their austere grin, their caustic gaze and merciless irony, the very conceit of hearing the dead speak, made and transformed into bony arrangements of biting remarks around being human — and who else better than the dead, to show the absurdities of life? Or Giacomo Leopardi's *Operette Morali*, a collection of metaphysical conversations which directly nod at Lucian in their restrained contempt, the alienation from self, signaled through voices other than self, other than world, other than plausible. I am drawn to those conversations between the living and the dead, the possible and the

---

6 This utterance echoes Harry Partch, "Revelation in the Courthouse Park," in *Bitter Music: Collected Journals, Essays, Introductions, and Librettos* (Champaign: University of Illinois Press, 1991), 342.

impossible, such as the dialogue of anatomist Federico Ruysch with a choir of mummies in his study, outlining an estranged space in a skillful rendition of flat, monotone, repetitive chant-like style speech; or Torquato Tasso conversing with a ghost, speculating on truth and pleasure, on humans "consuming life" between dream and fantasy to distract themselves from boredom, their ultimate inescapable condition.[7] Think, also, of the metaphysical dialogues of Edgar Allan Poe, "The Colloquy of Monos and Una" and "The Conversation between Eiros and Charmion," dialogues from the other world or after the end of the world, inviting to write even when the subject is otherworldly…

C.: *Otherwordy*.

L.: Even if only a shadow.[8] It has to do with the possibility of a conversation, even beyond death.

C.: Didn't we hear before, around here, of an *Infinite Conversation*?

L.: We did. Of reading as reverberation, reading that attends.[9] Importantly, we heard of the necessity "to learn not to develop"; to write the question that "insists but is not developed."[10] This appears to be a core form of D.C.'s study — one shaped as conversation rather than dialogue, as one Emile Bojesen remarked, where research is made as "plural speech" that seeks "strangeness rather than the confirmation and expansion of the known,"

---

7   Giacomo Leopardi, *Operette morali* (Milan: Feltrinelli, 1998).
8   Edgar Allan Poe, "The Colloquy of Monos and Una" and "Conversation of Eiros and Charmion," in *The Complete Tales and Poems of Edgar Allan Poe* (London: Penguin Books, 1982), 444–56.
9   Maurice Blanchot, *The Infinite Conversation*, trans. Susan Hanson (Minneapolis: University of Minnesota Press, 2016), 320–21.
10 Ibid., 339.

and can contribute to ways of finding, assembling, and transmitting knowledge that are many-voiced — [11]

C.: — and hold "the movement of thought."[12]

L.: A significant expression, "the movement of thought": it emphasizes transmission, a vitality in research that is never still, it animates language and how we think language in research. It shifts the attention on *being there,* on presence rather than progression, on the importance of being plural and thinking in the plural.

C.: The movement of thought is embedded in conversation —

L.: — in its undulating precision, Cristina Rovina wrote. Groundless but not without grounds, D.C. continued to echo.

C.: I am overjoyed. And I must interrupt.

L.: Aren't I surprised?

C.: I need a sudden shift.

L.: Subtle. Call it The Chimeric Catapult.

C.: I need to move to other characters who morphed their personae, in the plural: Robert Ashley with, respectively, Alvin Lucier and Pauline Oliveros in their hour-long conversations in *Music with Roots in the Aether,* the opera for TV that Ashley completed in 1976, consisting of a series of hour long interviews with seven composers and himself, along with as many performances. Allow me a lengthy quote from D.C.: *I watch* Landscape with Alvin Lucier *and my attention is not particu-*

---

[11] Emile Bojesen, "Conversation as Educational Research," *Educational Philosophy and Theory* 51, no. 6, (2019): 650–59.

[12] Ibid.

larly drawn to the discussion, but toward the combination of form and topic, when the form of the conversation becomes the topic, and one wouldn't be without the other. Ashley asks questions to Lucier who is dressed for fishing and is actually throwing fishing rods in the air, in a room. I wonder if the fishing rod is a tongue-in-cheek remark around the expression fishing for thoughts, *for linear fixed thoughts which will never inhabit the space of their conversation, filled instead with a high-pitched frequency. At first I notice it as unusual, then exhilarating, then definitely annoying, then I adjust to it and I'm intermittently reawakened to it. To claim to extract any text-as-meaning under such circumstances would be futile, as meaning is generated also by this intrusion, by the interruptions of common sense as it's teased by the interference of the frequency.* […] [N]ot knowing […] whether you got the idea that wakes you up at night from the hard-to-hear part of what comes over the radio, or from something you read about in a magazine about electricity, or from something you just dreamed up.[13]

L.: The conversation is not only with people, but with places, atmospheres, radio waves, dreams.

C.: D.C. goes on, Landscape with Pauline Oliveros *is* […] *a transformation, another way of deforming the closed space of the interview.* […] [W]*hile the conversation with Lucier was all flooded in a frequency which created an eerie urgency and restlessness, here the two seem to slowly sink, rather than think. After a drift of non-understanding and slow pacing, long pauses, thoughts stretched, anecdotes are taken on a ride around and never seem to come to a point. That's the point: to hover and hesitate, like the movements of the camera which takes turns to show and reveal other portions and presences which exceed the space of the interview yet inform them, little by little, emphasizing the hallucinatory quality of slow talk. Strange occurrences begin to unravel. A woman is ly-*

---

13 Daniela Cascella, *Singed: Muted Voice-Transmissions, After the Fire* (Prague and London: Equus Press, 2017), 84.

ing on a piano, surrounded by ropes and flowers. She is partially concealed. What kind of vision is this? Who is being summoned? Another mysterious woman wearing a mask joins Oliveros and begins to do her hair, makeup, nails […].

I've just witnessed a conversation that started with the intention of having no intention, and ends with a metamorphosis. A conversation that goes nowhere conventionally, and conveys a space for breathing-thinking. It drifts, reaches dead ends, wastes time and nonetheless makes meaning. It allows the unpredicted to surface, and be heard. At one point in the conversation Ashley, in his customary velvet tone of diffused thinking, partial self-mockery and partial vaporous intent, exhales words that go nowhere:

Does it allow for… does it allow for… do you… do you…

[…] [L]et words hesitate, waste time, spin around their meaningful nothing […]. Not to understand, but to do, Oliveros says. Not an extraction of meaning but a making through different manners and exchanges […] holding the sense of thinking, of drifting, through the aether, the medium that was once believed to fill the air and allow transmissions.[14]

L.: Conversation goes nowhere other than its csite, it deepens. Conversation also reminds me of the mystic *conversar* which, following de Certeau —

C.: — again, D.C. —

L.: — allows, between speaking and hearing, an "uncertain and necessary center" to appear; a "non place […] created by the stirrings the desire — "

C.: Chimeric.

---

14 Ibid., 85–86.

L.: "— for the other awoke within language, that is, by the reversal that emptied statements of their content in order to lay bare the prior question of the *conversar*."[15]

C.: And "because it concerned a practice, how things were said" mattered more and more.[16] Conversation only works if supported by a will to be there, which "founds a textual space amenable to the returns, the repetition and reversibility of reading. Upon the melting away of knowledge into will, it founds the didactic exposition of an itinerary."[17]

L.: It writes, and comments upon what it is writing, throughout. It writes, and lifts words off the page. It is tied to nothing —

C.: — and is similar to that quality which the anonymous writer of *The Cloud of Unknowing* called "naked intention," that is, being here because you are here and because you are so.[18] With no reward but, as Weil said, in a void "fuller than all fullnesses."[19] In a conversation "the disappearance of the content," D.C. continues, "and the exclusion of the past […] or future […] inflate the act of wanting itself. Originally, there is an absolute volitive, detached from anything known or possessed. It is the more powerful for being less determined by an object."[20]

L.: The verb is "tied to nothing."[21]

C.: As we need it.

---

15 Michel de Certeau, "The 'Conversar,'" in *The Mystic Fable: The Sixteenth and Seventeeth Centuries,* Vol. 1, trans. Michael B. Smith (Chicago: University of Chicago Press, 1992), 161.
16 Ibid., 164.
17 Ibid., 167.
18 A.C. Spearing, trans., *The Cloud of Unknowing and Other Works* (London: Penguin Books, 2001), 29.
19 Simone Weil, *Gravity and Grace,* trans. Emma Crawford and Mario von der Ruhr (New York: Routledge, 2002), 13.
20 de Certeau, *The Mystic Fable,* 169.
21 Ibid.

L.: It holds a "tending toward."[22]

C.: A chimeric yearning.

L.: A vanishing point.

C.: What happened to D.C., then? Last time I heard of her, she appeared lost in the hazy realm of *creative-critical* writing. Didn't she aim to *stain the accomplished forms of academic writing and present instead other fractured ways in which study can be articulated in words?*[23]

L.: She did, and the weight she carried inside was immense. Even though she had developed, over the years, something of an affection for cri-cre writing, she felt out of place. It became evident to her that while poets, performers, and art writers had long absorbed in their textual manifestations a desire for hybridity —

C.: A most dreadful term. Please say *chimeric,* it sounds better to my ears.

L.: — she realized that the critics largely continued to point at such hybridity —

[Chimera groans on hearing *hybridity,* as if tortured.]

L.: — while they remained entrenched in modes of writing that did not embody it. So D.C. felt like a stranger. But she continued to search for ways of writing, of thinking-in-writing, for approaches to the writing of research which could allow thought and words to be elsewhere, to be shaped in a way that allowed their form and cadence to sustain their arguments. Let me read

---

22 Ibid., 171.
23 D.C., unpublished quote from a lost book proposal.

to you from her notes, written one day when she attempted to appear serious, sincere, and straight.

[Chimera roars with laughter.]

L.: D.C. wrote, *The critic Irit Rogoff has proposed a definition of "embodied criticality"* —

C.: Just to hear it pronounced brings unease.

L.: — *as necessarily entangled. Neither criticism as distant judgement, nor critique as awareness of structures, "embodied criticality" generates meaning through connectedness with the materials that it studies.*[24]

C.: I gather D.C. was enthusiastic at the idea.

L.: Absolutely. Rogoff's acute observations informed and turned her understanding of possibilities for criticism beyond its boundaries. However, as D.C. noted, *The resulting writing does not reflect such connectedness, employing a distanced, formalized vocabulary which prevents the texture of critical writing from reaching the very entanglement it theorizes.*[25] Do you see? D.C. yearned for critical writing which would *practice* such entanglement and make it sound, informed by speculative and theoretical considerations, and at once animating its language —

C.: — as chimera. Hm. I suspect all she wanted was an excuse to talk about certain writers not usually considered and barely translated in English.

---

[24] Irit Rogoff, "What Is a Theorist," *Transformazium Log*, May 23, 2011, http://transformazium.org/log/2011/05/irit-rogoff-what-is-a-theorist/, and "'Smuggling' – An Embodied Criticality," *transform.eipcp.net*, August 2006, http://xenopraxis.net/readings/rogoff_smuggling.pdf.

[25] D.C., unpublished quote from a lost book proposal.

L.: — rather than imposing a formal structure that overwhelmed the individual, distinctive textures of her subjects.

C.: What kind of writer committed to their subjects would do such a thing?

L.: Someone more concerned with authorial coherence, I guess. You interrupted me once again. As I was saying, rather than imposing an overwhelming structure on her subjects, D.C. yearned for critical writing that would listen to them, speak with them, attempt to find, momentarily, shared grounds, no matter how unstable these may be in a conversation. She longed to show how critical writing may carry its arguments in and through the tones, rhythms, and registers of its subjects, from which it cannot be detached because entangled with them. She attempted, as a writer and as much as a teacher, to make a space, and a case, for practices of critical writing that experiment with multiple voices, questioning implied formal standards of cohesion when presenting critical reflections. As D.C. made a case for *the writing-hearing of criticism* as central —

C.: — and chimeric —

L.: — she presented it as a many-voiced transmission beyond the boundaries of text, understood and heard in yearning and excess, through listening and attunement. D.C. wanted more out of forms which, while talking eloquently and extensively about qualities of critical writing which are certainly chimeric, did not engage with them in *the practice of writing* to a point in which their very articulation would be enmeshed with their arguments. Writing as monstrous entanglement, instead of polished distant judgement, does not prove its arguments through logic but csites the reader by deepening, rotating, and echoing.

C.: Chimeric writing is critical, creative, and something more and something else than creative-critical. Tell me now, didn't D.C. have a degree in Art Writing?

L.: Yes, but again, at times she felt like a stranger in those lands. As a writer of criticism, for whom writing may have been an artistic practice as part of the metamorphosis necessary to find herself, but who would not identify in full as an artist, she reversed the Art Writing central tenet, defined by the Art Writing teaching team at Goldsmiths as a practice that "sustains all forms of art criticism."[26] Her writing did not sustain forms of art criticism: it was altogether criticism and practice, a practice at once artistic, critical, philosophical, and literary.

C.: Chimeric writing is art writing and something more and something else than art writing. I begin to understand the nature of D.C.'s operation, inhabiting these disciplines but never entirely tied to any. How about the essay?

L.: Any time she tried to write one, she ended up writing a deranged essay.

C.: That caused great amusement, and many rejections.

L.: Rejections also led D.C. to find the ways in which she truly could write, no matter how unpopular or untidy. She attempted to present ways in which chimeric writing may hold many forms together, while being something more and something else than creative-critical writing, something more and something else than art writing, something more and something else than an essay. It is there, and it is out of synch. In some cases, it even takes on forms not immediately perceived as critical writing, and it shows what else it can do, as criticism, by inhabiting such forms, chimerically. Now, you may recall how the essay was a widely practiced form in her days, for example in books by writers such as Anne Boyer, Brian Blanchfield, Kate Briggs,

---

[26] Maria Fusco, "11 Statements around Art Writing," *Frieze*, October 11, 2011, https://frieze.com/article/11-statements-around-art-writing.

Lisa Robertson, Eliot Weinberger;[27] all of them, in various ways, works of stylistic accomplishment, profoundly engaged with a multitude of formal possibilities, and often D.C. found herself having conversations —

C.: — often imagined ones —

L.: — with their authors, but —

C.: — her thoughts, and with them her words, were never fully contained in the essay form at a speculative and practical level. Moreover, as a stranger in English, how could she possibly aim for formal roundedness and flawlessness in her style? Her form was monstrous, implausible, held the sense of a yearning that entails unevenness.

L.: Chimeric writing is essayistic and writes something more and something else than an essay. D.C.'s essays were always inevitably deranged because they kept pushing her words outside their boundaries. Some may have been more rounded, others more awkward, reflecting the condition of strangeness in language, and the necessity to inhabit each form, even when not entirely in command of it, because the materials demanded them. The impetus of telling would override any concerns with style, and present the ugly, uncomfortable language advocated by Ingeborg Bachmann as the necessary gesture that disrupts literature toward critical forms of understanding.[28]

C.: A most telling case, Bachmann's. In her *Frankfurt Lectures* she continued to undo you and at once yearn for you. Literature

---

[27] Anne Boyer, *A Handbook of Disappointed Fate* (New York: Ugly Duckling Presse, 2018); Brian Blanchfield, *Proxies: Essays Near Knowing* (New York: Nightboat Books, 2016); Kate Briggs, *This Little Art* (London: Fitzcarraldo Editions, 2017); Lisa Robertson, *Nilling* (Toronto: Book*hug, 2007); and Eliot Weinberger, *An Elemental Thing* (New York: New Directions, 2007).

[28] Ingeborg Bachmann, *Letteratura come utopia,* trans. Vanda Perretta (Milan: Adelphi, 1993), 123.

is "never entirely fulfilled," she said, and continues to flee, and continues to prompt more writing. Literature is the space of the *not yet*.[29] It is chimeric.

L.: I flee for your sake. It is an un-measure I need, not a measure. A quality in the telling which makes my language fractured, impure.

C.: Even though Bachmann ended up talking a lot about you, her lectures were initially meant to be on poetics. I haven't completely grasped what made D.C.'s work a form of criticism rather than poetics.

L.: Charles Bernstein has stated that "poetics is the continuation of poetry by other means."[30] We may understand D.C.'s criticism as the continuation of her poetics by other means, in the chimeric space of yearning. The two terms are not antithetical. Her ambition was write a poetics of criticism, a manner of arranging and presenting critical reflections in which formal inventiveness and construction are as important as conceptual or theoretical claims. She believed, and it was a belief substantiated by practice and experience, that it is impossible to take singular histories of learning, and of individuation through reading, apart from the ways in which a work is understood.

C.: D.C., critic who moved through poetics. The tension in the term chimeric, holding a yearning of critical writing for art, poetics, sound, is crucial to understand her work, in motion and transmission, not fixity.

L.: An inclination toward the minor key, the faint signal; a drive to find, and found, a new vocabulary for her stranger-ness. Sometimes it is a drift, —

---

29 Ibid., 120.
30 Charles Bernstein, "Optimism and Critical Excess (Process)," in *A Poetics* (Cambridge: Harvard University Press, 1992), 160.

C.: — sometimes a ruin.

Cristina Rovina's Ruinous Drift into Nothing

The impulse toward writing commentary, Nicola Masciandaro has argued, proceeds by straying but never reaches so far to prevent from returning to the text that prompted it.[1] If the margin is the site of commentary, holding at once a tension for words to move away from the text they write around, and the impossibility for them to be entirely detached from it, the margin is also the site where boundaries may dissolve, a porous way of inhabiting text as self, and other. Masciandaro mentions Reza Negarestani's idea of *hidden writings* according to which there are no subsequent layers in the commentary of a text that demand straightforward interpretation of clear-cut material but seamless distortions. As they comment on a text, the commentators continue to write it.[2] "Commentary," Masciandaro maintains, "constitutes a structure of understanding and experience, i.e., consciousness. […] It is writing's way of staying original, in ever-new nearness to its earthly origins, in productive proximity to the fact that all writing is only on the earth. The *telos* of

---

1 Nicola Masciandaro, "Becoming Spice: Commentary as Geophilosophy," *Collapse, Volume VI: Philosophical Research and Development,* ed. Robin Mackay (Falmouth: Urbanomic, 2010), 32.
2 Ibid., 36–37.

commentary, its far-off end, is *tellus,* what bears us."[3] The margin allows text to exceed itself, and at once ground itself. The margin is a site. The margin bleeds. My margin, my csite, has tears and frayed edges. *Situs* in Latin is site as well as dust, mold, detritus, that deposit in a place across time.[4] To site is to be with residue, impure. My margin is where boundaries between site and cite, between being and reference, dissolve. I yearn for csiting that shifts writing away from pre-validated sources cited as fixed frameworks of legitimization, and sites itself as entangled and impure, claiming its singular being, citing its references no matter how obscure, and out of synch they may be. Csiting I cite and site, a porous way of being me not all me, quoting and placing, inhabiting text as self and other. Sometimes the text I csite is not exclusively on a page, it is spoken. Then writing that is csiting is listening is transmitting. Csiting I write, after listening to Elfriede Jelinek's Nobel Prize speech, of which I offer echoes and distortions, in part from memory, in part from what I wrote before, with her not all her, with gaps and missing links, from an aural margin, where writing flips into telling, where I yearn for writing, that speaks with its subjects, I hear the subtle noise of prose.[5] Listening to her speech the first time mattered, it continues to matter, growing beat inside my perception of writing in and out of the page, of radiance and discourse, presence and concealment. Something crucial is heard, not lyrical ornament, just because it cannot be summarized it does not mean it is devoid of substance. My commentary to this most profound and elusive piece cannot stay on the margins but inside, incsite. Where is commentary to a recorded speech? Where is the site, what is the csite in a spoken text so loaded and so ephemeral? It is not fixed. It is in hearing, in residue. For some time I inhabit it, for these pages I transform it, for ever I am transformed, into

---

3 Ibid., 37.
4 Roberto Calasso, *L'ardore* (Milan: Adelphi, 2016), 264.
5 Elfriede Jelinek, "Sidelined," Nobel Lecture, Swedish Academy, Stockholm, Sweden, December 7, 2004, https://www.nobelprize.org/prizes/literature/2004/jelinek/lecture/.

my fundamental cadence. Heartbeats in one cadence, questions of rhythm. Something had better remain unsaid, unsaid and groundless, groundless but not without grounds. It is spoken, I do not read but hear it, whisper it back to you, whisper the sense of being enmeshed in what came before in the history of my reading, those black ties, connections, states of voice, states of mind, states of mine, and the mine is deep, some of it unmapped, some of it dark, some of it with precious stones, some of it with dull rock and moss and useless damp slippery surfaces. I have dwelled there for long times, sometimes I have slipped. I never had I proper, had to construct my I my mine. Not having a voice mine means having to construct it, aware of the workings of rhetoric, artifice, assembling words found and connected by kinship, many voices, all mine. What came before and around I matters, broken material I have at hand, its cadence, never frame but heartbeat, core not score, heart not instruction. Even when there is apparently nothing to say. Listen. Some time ago, having found out about the other meaning of a song, I disappeared. I wanted to sing the song, not to say what it is. Is singing the gift of curling up, curling up with reality? What happens when there seems to be little real, realevant to sing? When a reality must be sung which is not current? My reality, my matter, my song is no formal thing. Sing? It can't be held in one style. The song that is another song cannot be tidied up and neatly arranged. Unruly, it tangles up with the work and words of other writers. What is it around my throat? A scar, the sign of necessity. How many slits, how many scars, to make my song heard. How many times retold, to make myself heard in that low hum, the subtle noise of prose, I heard. Read, heard? Read, heard, anagram plus the h of a breath. There I'll find the hum, heard in books, from those who were before, whom I can talk to without worrying about the right style, intent instead in finding kinship. The song may sound like an "abolished bibelot of sonorous inanity," in fact, it tells me my words.[6] It is me not all me, many voices, so they are,

---

6 See Stéphane Mallarmé, quoted by D.C. in "The Stain of Stein: For Chimeric Writing," *Tinted Window* 2: "Verbivocovisual" (November 2019):

unrulily, untidily, disturbing song, flip of a book, half slip of the tongue, rhyming words as much as rhyming a disposition with that of a dead one, the fractured voice of understanding, the same and not quite so. Words are my warders but don't keep an I on me. Listen. Here is what a wise reclusive one said to me: "What should remain, is always gone. It is at any rate not here. Still you must carry something for a long time, learn to be still, on site, csiting, sometimes even a short paragraph holds a long arc of time between one sentence and another. This is the portion given to you and you must attend to it, in the most dedicated manner, small as it may be. Get there late. Formulate your thoughts in the most brutal way, there is nothing left, nothing but a stone, a sigh, a spin, a song."[7] No, I do not worry. I cannot change much, I can transmit, transform this faint hum. It is cold here, it is the depth of night. So what is left to one, nothing but a stone, a sigh, a spin, a song.

93–100, and Allen S. Weiss, *Breathless: Sound Recording, Disembodiment, and the Transformation of Lyrical Nostalgia* (Middletown: Wesleyan University Press, 2002).

7 This quotation rewrites and distorts sections of Gottfried Benn, "Invecchiare: problema per artisti," in *Lo smalto sul nulla,* trans. Luciano Zagari, Giancarlo Russo, and Gilberto Forti (Milan: Adelphi, 1992), 307–35, merged with Jelinek's speech, and filtered through Cristina Campo, *Gli imperdonabili* (Milan: Adelphi, 1987).

Voice from a Faintspeaker: Remember how reading unravels after you have put down the book, in long stretches of time that exceed the actual time of reading, when thoughts coalesce and reach you unannounced. Remember the attraction you had for a page, a paragraph, a title, a cadence; the moment you realized you were there, inside those pages, and you were with their writer too. Read with your ears. Do not consider these pages only for what they are, but for what transmissions and conversations they prompt, what emotions they stir. Pay attention to connections across sounding elements, rather than evaluations of content. Criticism here moves elsewhere, into its assonance with crickets, into chimera, creature who never was.[8] Read these pages like D.C. reads the pages of others: allowing them to speak. Listening takes time, give these words time. They must be respected, not dissected. Do not expect lists or reports of outcomes. These pages are arranged with another type of knowing in mind, the one which in the Vedic texts studied by Calasso appears as *bandhu*: nexus, connection, bond;[9] the entangled form of knowing which Pizarnik yearned for in her journals as an intimate tie between the critic and her subject;[10] the circular knowing transmitted in myths, those most ancient forms of nonlinear arrangement of sensing-feeling-understanding, until in some points the discovery and awareness of the void converge toward a heightened sense of artifice.

Crackle. The voice from a faceless one, Maurice B., speaks for a few minutes. The voice from a Faintspeaker (bracketed in her muffled timbre but restless to be heard) stubbornly interferes with it to the point when it becomes difficult to distinguish who it is, who I is.

"[C]riticism — literature [criticism is literature, I take this as given] — seems to me to be associated with one of the most diffi-

---

8 "I am a creature that has never been." Vivian Darroch-Lozowski, *Voice of Hearing* (Toronto: Squint Press, 2020), 37.
9 Calasso, *L'ardore*, 171.
10 Alejandra Pizarnik, "4 Decembre 1962," in *Diarios* (Barcelona: Lumen / Penguin Random House, 2013), 536.

cult, but important, tasks of our time, played out in a necessarily vague movement [the necessarily vague movement in chimeric writing is a manner of attuning to the materials, of adjusting to a habit that does not always initially fit]: the task of preserving and liberating thought from the notion of value [what conversations might occur, if criticism is disjoined from judgement of value, and continues to call itself criticism?], consequently also of opening history [history in the sense that I carry, not only in my reasoning, but in my language, material and detritus that were before. How many dead writers are living in these words?] up to what all these forms of value have already released into it and to what is taking shape [*is taking shape,* present continuous; the shaping of a criticism as it is made; the making and changing of forms, as they are driven by different encounters] as an entirely different — still unforeseeable — kind of affirmation [affirmation, not failure; literature is not a *fait accompli,* Bachmann said.[11] It must be written. Stated and reinstated. Made. Criticism does not bestow opinions after the fact. It searches with the subjects of its study, and] this search is not only a theoretical pursuit, but it is the very process constituting the literary experience, and its possibility is constituted through testing and contesting, through creation. 'Search' is a word that should not be understood in an intellectual sense, but as an action taken within and in light of creative space. [Marvel at Blanchot's ante litteram illustration of 'practice-based research.'] Criticism turns what is not to be evaluated into the experience of the work. [I have thought, experimented with, and debated this chimera of Blanchot's, this criticism that turns what is not to be evaluated, into the experience of the work. I have found no other ways of achieving the experience of the work other than reading the work out loud, considering publication and distribution/transmission/diffusion as part of such experience, or, here's the crux, allowing my critical writing to enter the very fibers of the works

---

11   Ingeborg Bachmann, *Letteratura come utopia,* trans. Vanda Perretta (Milan: Adelphi, 1993), 22.

I am studying. This paragraph is my experience of the work *in writing, inside writing.*]"[12]

---

[12] Maurice Blanchot, "Preface, What Is the Purpose of Criticism?" in *Lautréamont and Sade,* trans. Stuart Kendall and Michelle Kendall (Stanford: Stanford University Press, 2004), 5–6.

My Chimeras

D.C.'s This-Curse on Chimeric Writing as Method

Let me tell you my story of Chimera. Not the one you will find in an encyclopedia of mythological figures. I trust you to be able to search for that one yourself, and readers who do not wish to move outside these pages, follow more or less legitimate hints and threads, contribute to diffuse the radiations of this work, and read more books, are not apt to approach these pages of excess. I will not tell you of Chimera's mother Echidna, of the monster's death by Bellerophon's lead spear hurled in her throat. I will not give you a concluded meaning, proper and clear cut, for myths and symbols never do. They are made of an elusive but present substance which does *not* get lost in translation and demands to be ceaselessly *transcelated* — at once transcending words, and carried in them, radiance and presence, cadence and glare — heard as tone, not carved in stone. I have something else to tell you, less straightforward, more necessary.

My chimera is endorsed by an eternity of transformations. It deliteralizes the idea of goal, stating with Hillman that the essential goal is instead the *opus,* the yearning inherent in doing.[1] It dismisses creative progression. It always existed and continues

---

1 See James Hillman, *Alchemical Psychology* (Putnam: Spring Publications, 2014), 232.

to change, like the alchemical *rotatio* whose task is not to move elsewhere than the material and deepen the understanding of it; like a myth, with its force of being grounded and different all the time, that is, all the time that may be given to the artifice and presence of its retelling.

I shall not quote the expected sources but give you my signifying reading practices that make chimera, here, in the material of my reading, reasoning, resounding. Remember one of the old myths of origin, the story of Prometheus, as told by Plato in *Protagoras*. Prometheus's brother Epimetheus is given by the Gods, who have just created the world, the task of assigning a quality to each creature. He leaves man at the end, is left with no quality to give him; in the attempt to patch up his brother's error, Prometheus steals fire. Origin lies in nothing left and in a stolen quality: there is no origin but in artifice, and the artificial stolen quality given to man is a substance that burns, the ardor of knowing.

The myth is mentioned by Bernard Stiegler in *How I Became a Philosopher* to introduce the idea of *hypomnesis* which, unlike *anamnesis* — the recollection of a memory — stands for the making of a memory, a figure of artifice.[2] The way in which each subject tells and constructs the story of their origin is driven by desire, Stiegler emphasizes — like Prometheus's attraction to fire, like chimeric yearning, like the Vedic ardor which is the means of knowing — and such desire is a *learned lack*: a node is perceived, significant and lacking ("nothing to say"), it is attended to and remade, over and over, like a fable which is present in its elusiveness, and continues to haunt us from childhood. Nothing is insignificant if it demands attention, if it sets you on fire, like the ardor of the Vedic ṛṣis who in their stillness and burning reached knowing. A desire for nothing echoes Weil,

---

[2] Bernard Stiegler, "How I Became a Philosopher," in *Acting Out,* trans. David Barison, Daniel Ross, and Patrick Crogan (Stanford: Stanford University Press, 2009), 15–16.

who studied the ancient Vedic texts, and wrote of desire without wishes for rewards. Chimeric is not the subject, not the object, but the yearning, the yearning for nothing, nothing yearning.

For Stiegler it is impossible to escape one's *milieu,* the substance in which each one is constituted, the locality of their language at once singular and enmeshed. There, a difference is perceived, which does not always appear but changes everything about the way a text is understood because of the way it is encountered, the specific way in which it speaks to one. Whatever is made meaningful — *made* meaningful in the uncovering of enmeshed singularity, not *pronounced* to be meaningful as diktat — it is so through *signifying practices,* sustained relations, across time.[3] How is a signifying practice brought into being? I think of Corbin's understanding of *creative prayer* in the context of his study of Sufi philosopher, poet, and mystic Ibn 'Arabi: prayer is not made to achieve anything but brings an existing relation into being as *unio sympathetica,* in the intensity and burning of "the creative power of the heart."[4] This form of prayer-practice is brought into being by assonance, by responding to certain encounters, the deep connections perceived in singular and sustained acts of reading through formal and tonal encounters. Their *because* has no causality, it is the necessary manifestation of kinship between a chimeric writer and the subjects of her study through their forms and resonant voices, always akin, always out of synch.

To bring chimera into writing I have coined the term *csiting,* conjoining *citing* and *siting* in an assonant desiring encounter; a way of working with texts beyond the rules of citation, a way of citing as hearing in reading, where I find my grounds as I read, site myself as I cite, go over the words that make my understand-

---

3   Ibid., 26–28.
4   Henry Corbin, "Of Unio Mystica as Unio Sympathetica," in *Alone with the Alone: Creative Imagination in the Sufism of Ibn 'Arabi,* trans. Ralph Manheim (Princeton: Princeton University Press, 1998), 120–35.

ing of chimera and these words are residual; *situs* in Latin is site as well as dust, detritus. As I csite I continue to ground, and unground residues. Here as I csite (hear my csite, hear my sight as I read) my sources are not my origin, understood in terms of a stable *before* that legitimates and authorizes what I write. They are not original, they are residual decaying and changing, they are beating hearts, cores of voices, rhythms and songs I heard before and continue to sing and they continue to beat. They are here, heard in the heartbeat of Clarice Lispector's "instant-now" of every reoccurrence, they are here, heard in the core of my understanding of Stiegler's signifying practices through reading-writing, they are here, heard because I hear.[5] They are the *artificed* meaningful substance made up from an apparent lack of quality, an apparent lack of words, that allows other words, other qualities to emerge.

A site for csiting. The geographical site in the region of Lycia in Anatolia where Chimera roamed, was a ravine extending up from the shore. I think of chimeric writing perched on a ravine, in Greek *krinein,* the root of *critical,* that discerns and leans toward and might fall into its yearning. It leans toward something else, a yearning perceived in the material of research, that separates and is at once medium for conversation. Chimeric writing is all, it is nothing, it is *krinein,* it is criticism, it falls into ravine, in Italian *crinale,* in English *crest,* that slides into *crestfallen,* a state of mind and again a fall, a ruin, *rovina,* ravine, fall, faint. All, nothing, oscillating between meanings found in sound, hearing in writing that ripples the surface of these pages, yearning for other ways of reading.

Chimeric writing is all, nothing, oscillating, a dynamic image. The dynamic image, for Bachelard…

---

[5] Clarice Lispector, *Água viva,* trans. Stefan Tobler (London: Penguin Books, 2014), 3.

Voice from a Faintspeaker: Rather than a direct reference to his work, I am tempted to offer you a reference to Pizarnik because this is how D.C. learned of Bachelard's dynamic image, that is, through a relay of fractured voices in those two writers, not a direct engagement with a primary source. All sources here are primary. There is not one abstract, even, universal underlying system of knowledge that is equal and reassuring in its stability. She learned to know from what other people told her in books, from overhearing, connecting, misreading, misled, reconnecting, and arranging according to the matrix of her specific thinking-feeling-being. In her specific understanding, Bachelard's dynamic image was forever tied to Pizarnik's understanding of criticism as "intimate tie."[6] D.C. was not concerned with what Bachelard said as fixed authority. She focused on what Bachelard *said to Alejandra* and, in turn, on *what she said to her,* in all our singulars that makes us *we*. She wanted to see *where else* that form of reading might lead her.

…the dynamic image, for Bachelard, is at once manifestation of a dwelling, and a changing.[7] It exists, and mutates. It csites. Composite and yearning, the various readings of Chimera, its various singular meanings, compose and open the form of study, never complete, always longing for something other than itself: the writing of this research, of this chimera, is never concluded. It is not only a dynamic image. It is, and has sound, voices that demand to be heard, meanings found in hearing. Research, resonance, residue; the writing of this research is built on residues that came before, and after the burning of chimera's fire-breathing operations, it leaves more residues, "for still hidden writings to read."[8]

---

[6] Alejandra Pizarnik, *Diarios* (Barcelona: Lumen / Penguin Random House, 2013), 536.

[7] Gaston Bachelard, *Lautréamont,* trans. Robert S. Dupree (Dallas: The Pegasus Foundation, 1986).

[8] Daniela Cascella, *En Abime: Listening, Reading, Writing: An Archival Fiction* (Winchester: Zero Books, 2012), 61.

Do not call Chimera interdisciplinary, do not call her hybrid: she will spit fire at you. Can you hear how differently chimera chimes? Chimera is an image, an image not seen, but an image imagined, heard in reading. Chimera — I understand from James Hillman as he writes of the deep forms of psyche which are manners of being in the world, of carrying presence every day — chimera is the way in which I see, not a content that I see; an image heard in reading that makes claims on me, and my task is not to interpret it, but to attend to its presence. Listen now, here is how Chimera met me, how I attended to it.

Chimera is the last word in Sonnet CXXIV by Gaspara Stampa, the Italian poet who in the sixteenth century wrote a cycle of *Rime* which disrupted the stylistic codes of Petrarchism by addressing her poems to women who spoke, felt, were in charge of their bodies and minds, rather than mute muses. Sonnet CXXIV is a song of lost love and a manifestation of the sense of being split, half alive half dead, feeling everything and feeling nothing. The writer's true form is "all and nothing, […] an image of Echo and Chimera."[9] I encountered the sonnet as it was named in a letter by the Italian writer Cristina Campo, who deemed it most exquisite, and who wrote of the necessity to write because nobody else had seen certain things the way she had, nobody had put them in conversation as she had.[10] I encountered the sonnet *after* I had realized that Chimera was to be at the core of my project, although I heard it in my yearning for chimeric writing before I knew what it was — how it was to form, perceived in its yearning, read as yearning, as much for what is there, as for what is not, one not strong enough, not sensed without the other — in my yearning, following up a thread of reading, Chimera appeared in the concluding verse of Gaspara's sonnet, sounding and speaking the sense of "all and nothing" that I perceive when

---

9   Gaspara Stampa, "Sonnet CXXIV," in *Rime* (1554).
10 Cristina Campo, "Lettera a Giorgio Orelli, Agosto 1954," in *Il mio pensiero non vi lascia* (Milan: Adelphi, 2011), 171; also mentioned in Cristina De Stefano, *Belinda e il mostro: Vita segreta di Cristina Campo* (Milan: Adelphi, 2002), 34.

I write, the loss of self, loss of sense, as dead, and in hearing Chimera summoning me in that last verse I was speechless, petrified, again, *Da Capo.*

Speechless petrified again *Da Capo,* rebeginning from an ending. *Pierre,* stone is the last word in the cycle of poems by Gérard de Nerval entitled *Chimeras,* among the masterpieces of Symbolist verse, poems dense in their vocabulary and transformative in their treatment of images. I encountered de Nerval's stone, certainly an alchemical one considering the writer's studies of the *opus,* as I was preparing to write to a friend, in an early attempt at outlining the idea of chimeric writing for someone beyond my private speculations. After mentioning my thoughts around stones and chimeras in my letter, taking a pause from writing, I opened de Nerval's book, and "a pure spirit beneath the skin of stones" summoned me from the last verse of the last poem, marking a rebeginning. I heard *pierre* vaguely rhyming with *Chimère,* stone rhyming with Chimera.[11]
Of course.
How couldn't it.
My ~~research~~ Chimera found me.
It found me as I was open to listening to it. Not only was I startled at finding out that my edition of de Nerval's *Chimeras* had been translated in English by Robert Duncan, whose *The H.D. Book* is one of the heartbeats in my work; but that a stone sits at the end of *Chimeras* gave a stronger orientation to my writing, and made it resound.

Stampa, Gaspara's surname, in Italian means print. For Eric Griffiths print "does not give conclusive evidence of a voice; this raises doubts about what we hear in writing but also gives an essential pleasure of reading, for as we meet the demands a text makes on us for our voices, we are engaged in an activity

---

11 Gérard de Nerval, "The Chimeras: Golden Lines" (1854), trans Robert Duncan, in *Aurelia and Other Writings,* trans. Geoffrey Wagner, Robert Duncan, and Marc Lowenthal (Boston: Exact Change, 1996), 164–65.

of imagination which is delicately and thoroughly reciprocal."[12]
Reciprocal, in voicing across the pages, are these pages, as "[t]he
intonational ambiguity of a written text may create a mute polyphony through which we [...] reflect on the inter-resonance of
those voicings."[13] Words here inter-resonate, between Stampa's
"senta tutto" and *"non senta niente,"* "I feel/hear all" and "I feel/
hear nothing" — *sentire* in Italian is at once to feel, and to hear.
My "true form / an image of Echo and Chimera," moving across
texts through their whispers and resounding connections, is the
true form of this writing.

In no prescriptive form do I want to say and write chimeric
writing, but in change. Its theory is not carved in, but made of
stone like the *teoria,* the procession depicted in the mosaics of
Byzantine churches. *Teoria* is motion suggested in the stillness
of mosaic *tesserae.* I want my theory to be like this: suggesting
movement, and at once, grounded to the core in the stillness
of its stone-hard *tesserae*; a procession that treads on slowly, by
degrees of attunement, in a stilling which is knowing-as-being-and-attention, in chimeric yearning.
It is still, and moves.
Only then may I write my *teoria,* theory that is material, thinking in the material of language and the transformations that
happen there.
A mosaic-theory made of stone is not always complete, some
of the *tesserae* are missing, so they must be imagined. It works
in excess of itself and its materials, into a yearning. Yearning
and excess for the untold unheard untranslated, with the fire
it breathes, the things that cannot be fully known but can be
sensed through the beautiful subterfuge of more words, so
when I write *chimera* no clear image appears but a muted blurry
symbol which continues to tell and continues to hide, which can
be told and retold in many forms, not forgetting the interfer-

---

[12] Eric Griffiths, *The Printed Voice of Victorian Poetry* (Oxford: Oxford University Press, 1989), 13.
[13] Ibid., 60.

ences. These pages cannot be an exhaustive overview of what chimeric writing is because chimeric writing is *not yet*. They are a singular proposition of what a chimeric disposition may effect, showing how it may animate researching, organizing research, writing research. Because chimeric writing is not a fortress but a ruin, you can find your singular way inside it, your echo, your chimera.

Chimera appeared, fleetingly, in a page in a previous book of mine, as I wondered how the voice of Chimera may sound like.[14] At the time I was concerned with multiple spoken voices; now I am drawn to voices temporarily held in writing, perceived in reading. It is never only a voice and a page, but it is a mesh of transmissions and conversations. Chimera reoccurred because one book opens another, and this writing of research unfolding through the years is never concluded, always residual, a-synchronous, always yearning, chimeric.

Chimera was the title of the opening poem in Dino Campana's *Canti orfici* (*Orphic Chants*), a collection of verses from the early twentieth century in which symbolism and lyricism merge with innovative rhythmic forms, and with attention to montage and unusual viewpoints. Chimera was heard in the rapturous and visionary voice of performer Carmelo Bene reading that poem, *"e ti chiamo ti chiamo Chimera."*[15] *Campana* in Italian is bell, a word contained in *libellula,* and Blanchot wrote that "perhaps commentary is just a little snowflake making the bell toll,"[16] so here is how my chimeric writing rings, hear how it rings. Chimera appeared in *La libellula* (*The Dragonfly*), a long poem by Ame-

---

14 Daniela Cascella, *Singed: Muted Voice-Transmissions, After the Fire* (Prague and London: Equus Press, 2017), 31.
15 Dino Campana, "La Chimera," in *Canti Orfici* (Milan: Rizzoli, 1989), 105–106; jokerfull, "Carmelo Bene – La Chimera (Dino Campana)," *YouTube*, December 1, 2008, https://www.youtube.com/watch?v=6dvlyfgLDZs.
16 Maurice Blanchot, "Preface: What Is the Purpose of Criticism?" in *Lautréamont and Sade*, trans. Stuart Kendall and Michelle Kendall (Stanford: Stanford University Press, 2004), 2.

lia Rosselli, who inhabited Campana's words and transformed them through misreading and not always correct rhyming, so that chimera becomes another composite, inappropriately but tellingly and soundingly echoing *sirena, chimera, sirena, e ti chiamo ti chiamo chimera, e tu suoni e risuoni chimera, sirena, and I call you I call you chimera, and you sound and resound chimera, sirena*.[17] Hear how Chimera glides over words across centuries, she will not be captured. It is Chimera, and in Rosselli's hearing it becomes *sirena*, siren. Sirens, Blanchot writes, are bearers of presence beyond present — the encounter which happens now and is always about to happen because it already has happened.[18] I read because I have already read, in the presence of a song still to be sung. It will have been heard.

Sometimes, rather than being present to the point of obsession in these chains of coincidences, echoes, and sonic metamorphoses, Chimera kept herself more muted. She appeared, unannounced and unassuming, in Book Eight of Apuleius's *The Golden Ass*, not doing much in the text other than being a secondary term of comparison, but secretly winking at me in recognition.[19] The appearance of Chimera on that page offered me a connecting link, a nexus with which to work, an unexpected endorsement of my study, another signal that my materials were coalescing around a profound core of thinking whose roots, or *antennae*, stretched far beyond myself. I was reading Apuleius while studying the Menippean satire, considering its form as a possible one for my work. A composite genre that emerged in the late first century CE mixing prose with verse, serious tones with parody and critique of canons, the Menippean satire contains fictional elements, but it is not a novel, Northrop Frye shows in *Anatomy of Criticism*. It "makes for violent dislocations in the customary logic of narrative [...] shades off into more

---

17 This sentence distorts some verses in Amelia Rosselli, *La libellula* (Milan: SE, 1985), 27–28.
18 Blanchot, "The Song of the Sirens," 105–13.
19 Apuleius, *The Golden Ass*, trans. P.G. Walsh (Oxford: Oxford University Press, 2008), 149.

purely fanciful or moral discussions, like the Imaginary Conversations or the 'dialogue of the dead'; the Menippean satirist, dealing with intellectual themes and attitudes, shows his exuberance in intellectual ways, by piling up an enormous mass of erudition about his theme or in overwhelming his pedantic targets with an avalanche of their own jargon."[20] Its form is crafted according to a tradition of exaggeration and artifice. Like the Chimera, it may seem impossible according to rules of consequence and causality, but it exists if other paths are taken, those of imaginative reading and learning. A polyphonic form *par excellence* — following Mikhail Bakhtin's arguments in *Problems of Dostoevsky's Poetics* — the Menippean satire allows to rehearse and contain a variety of voices and nonhierarchical points of view.[21] So I understood, this work would be written as a Menippean satire for critical writing, with exaggerations, incongruency, missing links, and sudden tonal shifts. Across interrelated sections — juxtaposing essays and lyrical prose, philosophical dialogues and commentary, from the rhapsodic to the meditative, from the declamatory to the parodic — its key arguments are not exhausted one by one in separate consequent chapters, but are unraveled throughout the text across its composite, polyphonic, monstrous, and impure form. It demands ways of reading equally varied and inventive.

Then my Chimera would reappear, as due, Da Capo. *To Each Their Own Chimera* is the title of a petrifying prose-poem by Charles Baudelaire in which the narrator encounters a crowd of curved desolate men, each bent under the weight of a Chimera with her claws around their chest, her head above each head like an ancient helmet, and moves on "prompted by an irresistible need to walk," considering the beast (perhaps, also, the best)

---

20 Northrop Frye, *Anatomy of Criticism* (Princeton: Princeton University Press, 2020), 309.
21 Mikhail Bakhtin, *Problems of Dostoevsky's Poetics,* ed. and trans. Caryl Emerson (Minneapolis: University of Minnesota Press, 1984).

part of themselves "with the resigned face of those condemned to yearn forever."[22]

Voice from a Faintspeaker: It is time in the underworld for D.C. to wake up. She recalls a nightmare. Not a good nightmare, not one of the memorable, disturbing, visually tempting ones but one of those mundane, missing-the-plane-could-not-catch-the-train nightmares; one during which, repeatedly, she was asked to clarify why she calls herself a critic. Over and over again. Her attempts at replying that these definitions are not entrenchments, but manners of placing oneself in a constellation; that she learned to know herself through a practice of critical writing, which does not mean her critical writing cannot exist in other contexts, in fact it was through the practice of critical writing that she realized she was a ruin, broken and imperfect, therefore porous to other open, unexpected forms… But what sort of questions were these? Is it necessary to continue getting tangled up with this chattering? Predictable sudden end to the nightmare: asphyxia. She tries to reply but is smothered, cannot speak, has nothing to say. The side effects of the Interdisciplinary Nothing? An overdose of Creative Criticism? We shall never know. Importantly for now she awakens in Hell. Chimera is by D.C.'s side. It seems apt to suggest at this point, how D.C.'s begins to sound closer and closer to…

D.C. [in a sudden fit]: …DECEASED! Corpsed in our proud school of critical writing, we can no longer write.[23]

C.: *Chacun sa chimère,* you once wrote.

D.C.: Ch-ch, Sh-sh. When I first read that prose poem, it seemed like a description of an imaginary painting by Gustave Moreau,

---

[22] Charles Baudelaire, "Chacun sa chimère," in *Piccoli poemi in prosa,* trans. Nicola Muschitiello (Milan: Rizzoli, 1990), 84–87. Translation by Cristina Rovina.

[23] Jerome McGann, *Swinburne: An Experiment in Criticism* (Chicago: University of Chicago Press, 1972), 8.

laden with a heavy symbolic spell and the menace of muddy oil paint punctuated with small slits of bright cerulean, gold, and crimson. I thought of the heavy threat, the dread I have sometimes in writing when I become very aware of the overspill, the lack of limit.

C.: The people in Baudelaire's piece are "tired and serious and grey."[24] This reminds me of you, D.C. You do not look healthy these days.

D.C.: I am exhausted, you know. Consumed by study, by yearning.

C.: Those people looked as if the beast had become part of them and continued to walk on "with the resigned physiognomy of those condemned to always hope."[25] Diabolic Charles, D.C., conjoining hope with condemnation. And you, with your exhaustion in the hope and condemnation of study.

D.C.: I'd rather carry a heavy Chimera on my shoulders and walk on, than become like the narrator at the end of the story, overwhelmed with indifference, and heavier than those people and their monstrous chimeras. Chimeric writing must be ugly when necessary. It must carry the form and sense of the exhaustion and the impossibility of completeness. This is why I never wrote a monograph. The dangers of falling into monomania…

C.: You are falling back into essay mode. I thought you and I had agreed it was not the appropriate way to proceed. Be polyphonic. The sick anxiety of ownership is too much for your feeble heart.

D.C.: Ah the noisy polyphony! You know well how I am drawn to making connections among disparate materials and diffusing

---

24 Baudelaire, "Chacun sa chimère," 84.
25 Ibid.

them. If certain words or turns of phrase did not inspire repellence, I would abandon my pursuit.

C.: And yet…

D.C.: And yet we are not afraid of beauty.

C.: Hush now. You should sleep now. I will bring you dreams of pure fruits that go crazy, of mad impurities.

Mad Impurities

by Cristina Rovina

It has become clear, in my reading, that in her later years D.C. wrote with chimeric yearning for Calasso's first book *L'impuro folle* (*The Mad Impure*), published in 1974 and not translated in English to date.[1] In her attempts to write around that book, having nothing to say about it, D.C. dreamt of *criticism as artificed and yearning creature that makes mistakes, impure*. She tried to show how, when Calasso writes of other writers he is, at the same time, writing about his own, not one without the other. Literature is read with chimeric yearning.

I want to study such yearning (that is, reading, writing, thinking) in its rotational spin, to hold a desire for words that makes me speechless, and to prove that this desire for nothing to say is the most profound site of attention, as Weil wrote: "[S]imply to desire it, not to try to accomplish it [...]. Attention alone — that attention which is so full that the 'I' disappears — is required of me."[2] This is the point when D.C. disappears. This is Weil's "point of eternity in the soul."[3] Once it is reached, there is "noth-

---

1   Roberto Calasso, *L'impuro folle* (Milan: Adelphi, 1992).
2   Simone Weil, *Gravity and Grace*, trans. Emma Crawford and Mario von der Ruhr (New York: Routledge, 2002), 118.
3   Ibid., 119.

ing more to do but to take care of it, for it will grow of itself like a seed. It is necessary to surround it with an armed guard, waiting in stillness."[4] Attention must not be attachment, Weil emphasizes. The focus should be on the study, not on the reward, "to desire in the void, […] without any wishes," a void "fuller than all fullnesses."[5]

Do not go lightly with Weil's words. As Calasso stated, they are ordeals, they need time, they are *impossible words* at once ancient, immediate, abused, difficult, those same words the French philosopher and mystic had encountered in the inexhaustible texts she kept returning to: Upanishad, Bhagavad Gita, the Presocratics.[6] Words such as love, necessity, desire, good, beauty, limit, sacrifice, void. I must suffer through them, weigh each one of them, before taking on the responsibility to write them. It is frightening to consider writing them, they can easily be mistaken as commonplace because they are fundamental. Dare I write beauty? Dare I write limit? Dare I write void? If I do, I step into the fire, and come out of it transformed. Weil's desire with no wishes or reward resonates with Calasso's insistence on *ardor* as the impetus for knowledge in Vedic culture, that is, the practice of *tapas* which was at once asceticism and heat, devotion and devastating blaze.[7]

I want to stay there, deeper inside the mad impurities and the ardor of my repeated readings of D.C. reading Calasso, shifting the site of commentary from a motionless mark in the margins to a movement *inside* the work and its substance, in change, in the same place and not quite so, csiting. In a plotless book of not-nonfiction that cannot be summarized, itemized, -ized, the words in excess can only move in other ways, as commentary is

---

4 Ibid.
5 Ibid., 13.
6 Roberto Calasso, "L'ordalia delle parole impossibili," in *I quarantanove gradini* (Milan: Adelphi, 1991), 361–65.
7 Roberto Calasso, *L'ardore* (Milan: Adelphi, 2016), 133.

formed in the sense of *making with*. The root of the word commentary, Masciandaro writes, is in the Latin *comminisci*: to create, to devise.[8] It stands for the creative act that goes with the work of reading, a motion of making something with the material of study, transforming.

L'impuro folle is a book about — no, "about" is not the appropriate term. In Calasso's books, in chimeric writing as I understand it from D.C.'s notes, *about* is never appropriate. It suggests separation, analysis appended, while any attempts at drawing an outline, a summary, end up in the frustration of having nothing concrete to hold, or account for. This is why D.C. did not want to reduce her subjects to case studies. There is a claim for accomplishment, result, samples under glass in the form of case study, while she wanted to shatter the glass, be and speak with the works she studied, in their doing and undoing; Gaspara Stampa's "all and nothing," D.C.'s chimera, where writing and reading are not *about* but *inside* and *with,* where D.C. found herself exactly where she started, understanding deeper the way in which she was there, the manners of being, the ways of perceiving, the sympathies which drew her to engage with certain materials.

A detailed study of the subject of *L'impuro folle,* Daniel Paul Schreber — the German judge and Court of Appeal president who chronicled his nervous breakdown at the end of the nineteenth century in *Memoirs of My Nervous Illness,* an account of psychosis through episodes of torture and voice-hearing, "nerve-language" and ray emanations, cosmic turmoil and sexual transformations that appeared in 1903 and that led Freud into developing his theories around paranoia — was never the point for D.C.[9] Having had enough of content, she was content with reading Calasso's book as primary source, on her own terms,

---

8   Nicola Masciandaro, "Becoming Spice: Commentary as Geophilosophy," in *Collapse, Volume VI: Philosophical Research and Development,* ed. Robin Mackay (Falmouth: Urbanomic, 2010), 45.
9   Daniel Paul Schreber, *Memorie di un malato di nervi,* trans. Federico Scardanelli (Milan: Adelphi, 1974).

hers not all hers because entangled with more voices, and now, with mine. To enter Calasso's book, read through D.C., I shall not consider its content but its title, and its blurb.

Title: *The Mad Impure*. Mad impurities, in a work of chimeras. It seems right, prophetic even. *The Pure Products Go Crazy* is the title of James Clifford's introduction to *The Predicament of Culture*, a book published over a decade after Calasso's, in which he merges ethnographical, museological, and literary analysis to study various conditions of uprootedness and displacement as forms of dwelling in the world that question given systems of authenticity. Quoted from William Carlos Williams, the phrase "the pure products go crazy" marks for Clifford a state of rootlessness, of ruin, that leads him to speak of self-ethnography rather than autobiography, to write the self as "perpetually displaced" and interfered with "a present of memories, dreams, politics, daily life," never rounded, whole, and detached from its *milieu*.[10] Calasso's *Mad Impure* is likewise an ethnography in which the impure self is made of literature and goes crazy; in which madness is the disruptive force that merges self and other, a disposition open to the impulse to collapse into the material the self resonates with and becomes, chimerically.

Calasso made an art of blurb-writing: his short texts printed on the inner flaps of the Adelphi covers are as legendary for many generations of Italian readers as the books they introduced. D.C. wrote extensively on her fascination with Adelphi in her Italian years, and on Calasso's blurbs, marginal and enigmatic texts *par excellence*, which place any introductory remarks away from the body of the text toward its material boundaries.[11] The blurb of *L'impuro folle* is significant to understand the book's chimeric

---

10 James Clifford, "The Pure Products Go Crazy," in *The Predicament of Culture: Twentieth-Century Ethnography, Literature, and Art* (Cambridge: Harvard University Press, 1988), 1–17.
11 Daniela Cascella, *Singed: Muted Voice-Transmissions, After the Fire* (Prague and London: Equus Press, 2017), 113–19.

qualities, and it is worth translating some excerpts along with Calasso's blurb of Schreber's *Memoirs,* published the same year. *L'impuro folle* is presented as a commentary that aims to reveal hidden threads which remained unspoken yet ran through the *Memoirs* like an invisible current whose effects were palpable, and present. "[A] contemporary oblique chronicler has laid out an initial report of such facts, which, so far, history books dared not mention"—a statement of ambiguity around who is speaking ("a contemporary ambiguous chronicler") and around the nature of the text (facts in a work of fiction).[12] I take the confusion of fact and artifice as portal into *L'impuro folle,* where the motions of transmission are more important than any stable assumptions of authorship, genre, or system. Even what is given as authentic cannot be trusted as such, Calasso insinuates: the reader will encounter "the authentic voice of the President who talks, narrates, makes notes, reflects, oscillating between various apparitions, from the glorious one in the role of gnostic Sophia to the more somber one of retired Saxon magistrate. […] [H]e still wanders among us."[13] The authentic voice is many-voiced; it wanders in the present.

The final section of the blurb is no less than a declaration of method, from which D.C. derived hers: "The author of this book, concerned most of all with staying faithful to the news he had set out to transmit—abnormal news because, contrary to use, the news is in itself a form—could not narrate this story, contaminated since its origin, unless by following a process of continuous contamination."[14] The book is a transmission of news, the news is the form, the form is contaminated, so its writing is contaminated too. This method forms these pages, this is chimeric writing.

---

12 Calasso, *L'impuro folle,* inner coverflap.
13 Ibid.
14 Ibid.

I read *news,* the Italian *notizia,* in relation to the Latin *notitia,* that is, knowledge which announces itself, demands to be noted, and which one gains full acquaintance with through close scrutiny, the opposite of careless scrolling through. I want to drift now, interfere with *notizia* on a level which may seem superficial but discloses other ways of reading, and understanding. Impossible to resist the hint, as I am commenting on the writing by someone like D.C. who made a body of work from assonance, pun, and rhyme. *La notizia intorno a Didimo Chierico* (*News around Didimo Chierico*) is a short text the Italian writer Ugo Foscolo published in 1813 as an introduction to his translation of Laurence Sterne's *Sentimental Journey through France and Italy,* where Didimo Chierico appears as the semi-fictional translator. Foscolo describes Didimo as a character who no longer wants to write, and for whom life has the "heat of a far-away flame."[15] I find it difficult to ignore that D.C. shared her initials, and I suspect more than that, with Foscolo's disillusioned character. Didimo also appears as the author of Foscolo's *Didymi Clerici Prophetae minimi Hypercalypseos liber singularis* (*Singular Book of the Hypercalypses of Didimo Chierico, Minimal Prophet*), a satire against corruption in the literary world and in support of intellectual independence, written in verse in the manner of the Apocalypse, and published in 1816 in two editions; ninety-two copies for sale and twelve for Foscolo's friends. Deemed impossible to read because of its obsolete language and obscure references, Foscolo's text holds concealment in its title (*kalyptein,* to cover, *hyper-,* exceedingly) and has a Vision as its core part, just like D.C.'s work. In the years before her disappearance, she often mentioned that she was only writing for a handful of friends, those "twelve readers who can give attention and respond," a position not dissimilar from Didimo's, his book's few copies, and its mystifications.

---

15 *Wikisource,* s.v. "Notizia intorno a Didimo Chierico," 1813, https://it.wikisource.org/wiki/Notizia_intorno_a_Didimo_Chierico.

Back to Calasso's book. The *notizia* around the Mad Impure, reported by the "oblique chronicler," begins with the declaration of "a tear in the order of the world," and follows with a distorted version that rewrites the opening pages of Schreber's book. It is difficult to locate a stable narrative voice: the reader encounters, early on, a reference to "the celestial chronicler, the witness-actor," the former of which may be referred to Schreber himself, the latter to the writer of the book who often falls into the words of Schreber. Notes are given on the abandonment of subjectivity, on dualism (or is it duality, in the gnostic sense of two levels of understanding not opposed to each other, but coexisting?) merged with nods to hidden knowledge. By the time I reach page 28 I am adrift, no longer sure who is writing, who is the source of information, which are conjectures around existing documents, what is document, what is documented when the material is taken from memoirs which are undeniably impure. Contaminated since its origin, this chronicle cannot be told unless by further contamination, sudden changes of tone, switches in register and form: appellation, report, chorus, verse, gnostic imagery, reported speech, an oneiric vision in the manner of Jean Paul, the early Romantic poet who coated his words with a desolate air of otherworldliness and visionary convulsions. In a lunar atmosphere that suddenly haunts a handful of pages — one of Calasso's typical anachronistic twists — Jean Paul appears in *L'impuro folle* as a splendid interference, stating that his only scope in life was to capture the words of others, and merge them with vagueness. For Calasso, and for D.C.'s chimeric writing, it is an inhabitation of tone, rather than an exercise in quoting words. His *oeuvre* can be read as a sustained inhabitation of the prose of others.

After a handful of pages that report the speech of Paul Flechsig[16] inaugurating his Rectorate at Leipzig University — I am not sure if the speech is entirely or partially lifted from docu-

---

16 Paul Emil Flechsig was the nerve-cutting psychiatrist who treated Schreber and whom the judge maintained was in control of his torments.

ments, or entirely or partially invented, and at this point it no longer matters — page 57 initiates a ruinous descent into impurity, which becomes sovereign matter of the book. Impurity in language enmeshes, while showing Schreber's reader, the ambiguous chronicler, enmeshed in language. Schreber speaks to Calasso and in doing so the two are distinct and together, them not all them, disrupted by interference and otherness, bonded by words, by the inner voices that constitute a reading being; in this book, the voices of Jules Michelet, Sir Thomas Browne, Marianne Moore, Emily Dickinson, Tristan Corbière, Lautréamont, Arthur Rimbaud, *The Song of Songs,* gnostic texts. At times these are arranged polyphonically, at times as soliloquies, woven into the fabric of the text, often out of synch with it, unquestionably artificial, left in their original language, mistranslated, mixed with other words drawn from a murky reservoir of literary reverie. On page 66 Schreber is transformed into the gnostic Sophia. Knowledge is gained after having gone through all those materials, impure and attuned, only to prompt another process, another transformation, another yearning. The more delirious and tangled the book becomes, the more as a reader I am transformed. I learn to perceive connections, and on rereading the book I look at words differently, I could write otherwise. At the end of the book, in a switch to a more subdued tone, Schreber appears as a retired man wandering the world, haunting places, and visiting old friends such as Tiresias, Gottfried Benn's Ptolemaic, Karl Kraus. He is last seen in a pub in Charing Cross and is lastly documented among the Schizophrenic Anonymous in Canada.

Interspersed with hidden quotations and csitations, *L'impuro folle* appeared long before the internet search made it easy to trace their references. In 1974 the book asked to be read in the inaccessibility of its sources, because of their inaccessibility. The unevenness of its texture — voices in other languages, sudden breaks and reprises — asked the reader to perceive that something else was there, beyond the immediately available text, something whose pulse could be perceived before it could be known, and whose substance was at once present and not entirely manifested. The opposition between being and not being, presence and absence, understood in the canon of Greek philosophy, cannot be applied to Calasso's pages — here *not being* is Vedic, not void; it is another form of presence lodged unstably in the excess of material.[17] To know is the ability to see the connections between what is manifested and what is not, the tension between the two.

The apparent opacity of *L'impuro folle* invites me in. It is not a distancing device, but it includes me, unless I expect to be told everything in one reading. *I will never comprehend the entirety of Calasso's knowledge, but I cannot let go of the experience of searching, of learning with it,* D.C. wrote. Even if she could have interviewed Calasso in her lifetime, to ask him about the role of hidden quotes in his first book, D.C. chose not to. *Asking him,* she noted, *would be like asking Dante to clarify what he wanted readers to believe Ugolino did, or did not, in the Tower of Hunger* — a statement that recalls Borges, writing of Count Ugolino's ambiguous cannibalism: "[Dante] did not know any more than his tercets relate. [...] Ugolino devours and does not devour the beloved corpses, and this undulating imprecision, this uncertainty, is the strange matter of which he is made. Thus, with two possible deaths, did Dante dream him, and thus will the generations dream him."[18] There are experiences which are present and unspoken in literature, and their presence is not evidence in the form of hard fact, but "undulating imprecision." D.C. was content with the evidence, full and wavering, that reading provides, and called its undulating imprecision chimeric.

---

17 Calasso, *L'ardore*, 169–71.
18 Jorge Luis Borges, "The False Problem of Ugolino," in *Selected Non-Fictions*, ed. Eliot Weinberger, trans. Esther Allen, Suzanne Jill Levine, and Eliot Weinberger (London: Penguin Books, 1999), 278–79.

In the case of Jelinek's play *Her Not All Her,* which employs the words of Walser as material without direct attribution of sources, the lack of referenced quotes makes the reader participant in the material of the text, and at once claims for the impurity of the text to be taken as such — not legitimated, not sanctioned, only read, only studied, and that only is plenty. As I read Jelinek's play I hear Walser because I have read Walser before, I sense recognition in my reading, a form of entanglement. What happens though if it is not Walser's work to be used as material, but texts whose presence is more elusive, whose signal is more faint, like in the case of those in *L'impuro folle*? It is unlikely that a reader will recognize every hidden quote. The term of comparison is the singular one built from Calasso's own reading and study, which barely has any echo because few will have read what he has read. As I read I perceive little recognition, other than intermittent glimpses of familiar verses learned by heart many years ago and reappearing here distorted, but a sense of estranged presence, and at once, a restless yearning to search for those texts, to find my bearings. Gradually I introduce my own references into the reading, no matter how hidden, or out of synch with Calasso's they might be. This is exploratory, irreverent, chimeric. Because I am not given a compass I must find my way, as the presence of quotes in Calasso's book is not a system of legitimization. Here I learn to read, relying on my resources and on my sources, I learn to find my movements in unfamiliar words, in the lack of references that would allow me to feel safe. Calasso does not want his readers to feel safe. He wants the experience of reading to convey the same destabilizing experience of loss of self, the "tear in the order of things" that Schreber's memoirs represented for their readers. He wants his readers to feel unbalanced, not protected, because this is knowing, and this is how D.C. thought the writing of research may be shaped, groundless but not without grounds. It is not a threat but a shift in perception. The book escapes signifying because its sense cannot be entirely held. It demands to take those quotes *in reading* as contributing to the fabric of knowing. If I choose to resist the immediately revealing internet search, I am left perceiving unevenness in a prose full of interferences and distorted signals nonetheless heard. Like Schreber's body, the book becomes a transmission device. An unsettling sense of impurity inside the boundaries of the book is matched with a sense of alterity, of language built from others, resounding other voices.

Here is the only extant fragment of D.C.'s essay on *L'impuro folle,* in which she aimed to show how the book could be read as the csite of transformation at the heart of Calasso's writing:

In the blurb Calasso writes that the only form apt to contain the story of Schreber was the "most impure form": the novel. Contrary to this statement I want to read L'impuro folle *not as a novel, but as a critical work that embodies the poetics and the fictions it studies, that yearns for the substance and material of its inquiry, critical and fictional: chimeric. There seems to be a resistance in the book, as in all of Calasso's work, to assume criticism and commentary as detached forms of engagement. I read the resistance as a way to regain criticism by other means: as resonance, in the sense of Blanchot, as inhabitation, as in the body of the mad impure. When he published the Italian translation of Schreber's* Memoirs, *Calasso accompanied them with a long text which was not a canonical critical study or introduction, but a survey and evaluation of the critics of the* Memoirs: *he places himself at further remove from the text, writes a critical study not of the book, but of its critics. Where is Calasso, critic of the* Memoirs, *to be found then? Inside* L'impuro folle. *This is the news, the "shocking news" that lodge in the form of the book. If I take Calasso's understanding of critical writing as the ability to capture "that most mysterious parameter which no semiological grid has been able to capture so far, and for good reasons: the timbre of an author," then I read L'impuro folle as a work of critical writing in the shape of a fiction, in which the transformation of the writer's voice into the timbre of the (many-voiced) object of study occurs.[19] With the excuse of publishing a translation of the* Memoirs *Calasso began*

---

19 Calasso, *I quarantanove gradini*, 306.

a transformation: he knew that writing about Schreber's book did not mean to learn, but to suffer it. Another double emanated from the pages, something is decomposed. A sinister euphoria pervades the process. What is writing, in this undulating delirium?

The critic's choice in front of the works he loves best, Blanchot writes, is either to be in *silence,* or to conjure a form of writing that does not judge or observe from a distance, but offers *the experience of the work.* The necessary gesture in chimeric writing, D.C. says, is not to understand silence and experience in opposition, but to imagine and practice a writing of *experience with silence,* in being and listening, enmeshment and study, that lodges unstably in inhabitation and haunting as well as in stillness and contemplation. For Blanchot, "[t]he critic is by nature on the side of silence."[20] For D.C., the critic is by practice on the side of writing. If silence is her nature, then writing is her opus, and as such, it acts necessarily and alchemically *against nature* as the *opus contra naturam*: practice against nature, the artifice necessary for a transformation.

Against nature, monstrous, like Chimera. In the Middle Ages stone monsters were placed at the edge of cornices and buttresses, symbols of uncontrolled forces relegated into the decorative space. But there is little decoration, let alone playfulness, in forces and symbols that cannot be pinned down. They are necessary. Chimera-monster does not play with words. "I am not playing with words," wrote Clarice Lispector in *Água Viva,* "I incarnate myself in the voluptuous and unintelligible phrases that tangle up beyond the words."[21] D.C. carried this sentence with her across two books and countless public readings, pinned it in front of her desk, learned it by heart. Not playing with words: the engagement with the textured impurities of lan-

---

[20] Maurice Blanchot, *Lautréamont and Sade,* trans. Stuart Kendall and Michelle Kendall (Stanford: Stanford University Press, 2004), 46.
[21] Clarice Lispector, *Água Viva,* trans. Stefan Tobler (London: Penguin Books, 2014), 15.

guage is attentive, significant. It laughs, aware of its nothingness, and committed to it. It is never *playful* in the sense of superficial, whimsical, passing. It is not playful in the sense of the alarming distinction often posed between creative writing practices as *fun* and critical writing as *serious*—a problematic statement that corners critical writing in a negative realm of boredom and *work to be done,* and at once implies that *lack of fun* is guarantor of engaged work. Chimeric writing is poetic work embodied in voluptuousness, in the substance of its subjects. It is committed, not only in its engagement but in the moments of study that have nothing to say, in repetition and locked grooves, in substantial boredom as much as irreverence and laughter. To separate the committed aspects of any work from the playful ones diminishes both, denies the entanglement of the two, dismisses the value of non-eventfulness and the critical substance of play. Eileen A. Joy proposes the expression "weird reading" to highlight how pleasure and enjoyment "can be an importantly ethical matter, especially in academic disciplines (literary studies, historical studies, philosophy, etc.) that are often suspicious of pleasure and enjoyment, privileging instead what some term 'strong,' 'skeptical,' 'sober,' 'serious,' and 'rational' critique."[22] The same point can be made for chimeric writing, while stating that uneventfulness, boredom, repetition, and obsession also have a part in ideas of criticism expanded from the limitations of terms such as "productivity" and "purposefulness." Nothing to say is plenty, the desire for nothing is full… of faint signals.

Calasso sweeps over the works and ideas he writes about, forms visionary statements, connections unheard of before, grounded on extensive research but arranged in ways that resist the exhaustive account while offering a strong sense of having inhabited those works for a long time, *otherwise it would not be possible to write like that.* A deep intent runs through the pages to show that knowing occurs through connections and associa-

---

22 Eileen A. Joy, "Weird Reading," *Speculations: A Journal of Speculative Realism* 4 (2013): 28–34.

tions, slippages and sudden turns, which prose must embody rather than deny or tidy up in a consequential arrangement of questions/demonstrations/conclusions because "the history of ghosts is more indispensable than facts" and ghosts haunt, distract, cannot be silenced, or regimented.[23] No *mad impure* would have been written or heard without the other voices that haunt it, dismissing any possibility of exhaustive knowledge and making more prominent the exhaustion of chimeric yearning.

Twenty years after *L'impuro folle,* Calasso published a collection of short texts and reviews by Giorgio Manganelli, where I believe he heard echoes of himself and the many voices populating his books. In one of the texts, entitled *Ma Kafka non esiste (But Kafka Does Not Exist),* Manganelli reviews Piero Citati's book on Kafka, condemned at the time for not being a proper work of criticism.[24] It is an *impure* book, he writes. Mixing biography, narrative, summary, conceptual considerations, letters, journals, aphorisms, it looks like a private project with Kafka as theme. "I am convinced," Manganelli states, "that criticism is simply literature about literature. Criticism does not explain, does not judge [...], does not find values, has nothing to understand; it is an arrangement of words about words."[25] He continues, "The rigour lies in the route that links a number of quotes [... A] critical text is made equally of presence and absence, quotes and omissions, day fragments and night fragments. The idea that exhaustive criticism can exist is as wise as the claim that an exhaustive sonnet exists."[26] I want to emphasize the following: "Criticism does not have an ancillary task to so called creative literature but, despite its limitations — analogous to those of a *sestina* — it is itself creative, therefore impure: because it uses words, and words are impure: words hold a nocturnal

---

23 Calasso, *L'impuro folle,* 329.
24 Giorgio Manganelli, "Ma Kafka non esiste," in *Il rumore sottile della prosa* (Milan: Adelphi, 1994), 118–21. Translations by Rovina.
25 Ibid., 118.
26 Ibid., 119.

presence, and this verbal *blackitude*²⁷ is the mark [...] of literature. [...] Using the words of others inside the cocoon of its own, [criticism] introduces obscurity where is illusory clarity, [...] captures and treasures the mistake where apparently there is pertinence [...]. [The critic] has the task of an enchanter: to make drawings, hexagons, argyles, saint Catherine's wheels out of those mysterious nocturnal animals [that he studies] — incidentally, I ignore what exactly the *artificed*²⁸ figure might be, [...] invented under this name, but we have already said that literature gives herself up to the steady hold of irresponsibility."²⁹

As I read the above, I kept hoping and not hoping that Manganelli would write *chimera*. Hoping, because his words resonated so profoundly with my thoughts around chimeric writing to the point when I could feel they recognized me. Not hoping, because I wanted to take those words elsewhere, slightly farther away from themselves to the only place they could be, to the csite of my understanding of chimeric writing, built from the words of others and yet adding the unruly weed of its uneven growth to the ruin of all the literature that came before me.

George Steiner states that as critics in front of a work, our instruments are blunt.³⁰ Perhaps they need to stay blunt, and there is no need for critical writing to cut anything. I can move differently, draw closer to the work, not by means of sharp instruments, but listening, merging with it, and finding myself many-voiced, *artificed*, impure, chimeric.

---

27 Rovina's translation of the oddly sounding Italian *nerità*.
28 Rovina's translation of the oddly sounding Italian *artificiata*.
29 Manganelli, "Ma Kafka non esiste," 120.
30 George Steiner, "Whorf, Chomsky and the Student of Literature," in *On Difficulty and Other Essays* (Oxford: Oxford University Press, 1978), 137–63.

Imaginary Conversation

D.C. and Chimera

Voice from a Faintspeaker: Consider D.C. talking to Chimera, a disappeared character talking to her yearning, to an impossible audience of one. D.C. is dead, Chimera never existed. All, and nothing. What to do in front of nothing, in front of a voided expectation? Laugh. Hear the laugh of Chimera, read D.C.'s écriture chimerique.[1]

C.: Still speechless, D.C.?

D.C.: As speechless as _____ [chokes].

C.: Still interdisciplinary?

D.C.: I'd rather be interred.

C.: Did I hear interned?

D.C.: Better to call me mad than a *prose stylist* — a stylite, perhaps. Leave me on a pillar, to rot. The study of that rotting

---

[1] A nod at Hélène Cixous's essay "The Laugh of the Medusa," trans. Keith Cohen and Paula Cohen, *Signs* 1, no. 4 (Summer 1976): 875–93, in which she proposes an *écriture féminine*.

unspeakable substance underlying language, which Amelia Rosselli made evident in her poem *La libellula* through slight repetitions and variations of misspellings, absorbs me a lot more that any polished surfaces. And do not call these thoughts old: they are significant.

C. [not quite sure who and what she is responding to]: But do they have any meaning? Careful with generalizing. Plus, that phrase you have just said is stolen.

D.C.: So what? My remark is not any the less pointed because it is not perfectly original. It holds and presents the way I think, as it goes in and out of *just words*. Somehow the words I use are props. Or call them baits, fishing for whatever is not word. Sometimes these books I inhabit, these texts from which I take words and sentences, feel as if they have grown on my body like a beak or wings, in a metamorphosis.

C.: I begin to see your canny move. Not only are you satisfied with inhabiting those texts so you may articulate, or shall I say usurp, your extravagant forms of critical writing. You also want to inhabit their methods, the way in which writers moved into and out of their words, thought of them, inside and outside of them, were exhilarated and exhausted and exasperated by them. Pasolini for example, who instead of quoting manifestly from Lucian's *Dialogues of the Dead,* inhabited one of them to the point that it became part of his work, not framed as quotation, but integral to the text's movement and cadence, his not all his. In turn you haunted that same dialogue some time ago and made it an integral part of your work. How does it make you feel?

D.C.: It makes me feel less alone.

C.: How so?

D.C.: I am thinking of the subtle and profound understanding reached in those instances of contact that happen at times during attuned reading. Those moments in which a text appears as "the most naked and charged of life-forces."[2] In this state, books are "not 'sources' in any formal auxiliary way, but bodies of lived meaning, animate spaces of understanding and emotion" in which we "register our own pulse."[3] This form of intimacy gets to the core, it is more profound than the physical, it is frightening sometimes.

Frightening [the voice of William Carlos Williams takes over the Faintspeaker]: "You have turned me inside out [...]. We don't in this world admit such intimacies, we have to hide them from each other, but you have found me out, I am frightened by it..."[4]

[Chimera shivers, she is frightened too. She feels she is being touched by some piercing and ancient sensation she had not experienced since the time in which Mechthild von Magdeburg, the Beguine, wrote of that most chimeric dance of the soul and the senses, in a voice overloaded with pain and love, and from love to knowledge, and from knowledge to desire, and dance, dance.][5]

D.C.: Do you begin to understand? I am talking of the urgent, exhilarating coagulation of ideas that happens in private, in moments of thinking-with-reading; of the conversations with the absent ones, that touch so deeply, and are so present. The question is no longer, "have you read that book?" but, "have you been there?"

---

2 George Steiner, "Dante Now: The Gossip of Eternity," in *On Difficulty and Other Essays* (Oxford: Oxford University Press, 1978), 176.
3 Ibid., 177.
4 Monica Farnetti and Giovanna Fozzer, eds., *Per Cristina Campo* (Milan: All'insegna del pesce d'oro, 1998), 107.
5 Mechthild von Magdeburg, "Rivelazioni," trans. Antonio Ballardini, in *I mistici dell'Occidente,* ed. Elémire Zolla (Milan: Adelphi, 2010), 2:774–79.

C.: With its spirit…

D.C.: With the spirits that can form out of books, like the ghost in that Japanese story who appeared in the eyes of the reader by means of a deep sympathy.

C.: I remember that story, "The Sympathy of Benten," as retold by Lafcadio Hearn. That moment when someone who was thought as lost, is recognized again through reading; the same person, but slightly out of synch with the world. "The same — yet not the same. When she wrote […] something of her spirit passed into [the words]. Therefore it was possible to evoke from the writing the double of the writer."[6]

D.C.: From now on I shall use the expression *I have hearn,* instead of *I have heard,* any time I want to convey a sense of hearing-in-reading, in conversations even when impossible or inaudible, a perception of voices inside and beyond the page, voices beyond reason felt and heard, hearn.

C.: The story by Hearn may only be understood by rejecting the safety of evidence and embracing mystery — not in a shallow sense but in the sense Sir Thomas Browne intended it, as substance of the unspoken material which haunts words, perceived at that point where there no longer seem to be any words: "I love to lose my selfe in a mystery, to pursue my reason to an *O altitudo*."[7] Yet words are written, to convey the ineffable perception of altitude, and they must be arranged. Mystery needs Manners, two terms matched by Flannery O'Connor in her understanding of writing that could only reach beyond words through an engagement with words, and attention to their forms. She

---

[6] Lafcadio Hearn, "The Sympathy of Benten," in *Japanese Ghost Stories* (London: Penguin Classics, 2019), 85.

[7] Sir Thomas Browne, *Religio Medici and Hydriotaphia, or Urne-Buriall,* eds. Stephen Greenblatt and Ramie Targoff (New York: New York Review of Books, 2012), 12.

spoke of qualities that endure, most hidden and extreme, which can only be conveyed by awakening to every single word written. She said that to apprehend a form through attentive reading, means to contemplate the mystery embodied in the whole work.[8] Mystery, manners: you may also recall how, instead of referring directly to the Eleusinian Mysteries, Pasolini made his book *Petrolio* an embodiment of the very metamorphoses at the heart of those ancient rituals.

D.C.: At Eleusis the rituals of transformation in the Mysteries were toward a very specific form of knowledge, not one aimed at discovering hidden things but "the secret of that which lies in front of everyone."[9] You see what has always been there, but your perception of it has changed.[10]

C.: So writing, that comes from reading, has to do with *staying there* and scrutinizing what you have collected in front of you, by sympathy.

D.C.: And *there* is the csite where a mutation into oneself is suffered. Initiation is fulguration, contact.

C.: Many things to laugh about, and many grave things. Remember, at the center of the rituals of Eleusis was transformation as much as laughter. Demeter, in the darkest depths of sorrow for her lost daughter Persephone, at one point, cyclically, laughs. There is emphasis, in your project, on the potential of laughter as excess, uninhibited exaggeration, wildly imaginative wordplay, all of them legitimate and committed modes of reflection. Or are you laughing at your inability to write straight to the point?

---

[8] Flannery O'Connor, *Mystery and Manners: Occasional Writings* (New York: Farrar, Straus & Giroux, 1970).

[9] Roberto Calasso, *Il cacciatore celeste* (Milan: Adelphi, 2019), 416.

[10] Ibid., 424.

D.C.: Let's say "reverberance" instead of "reflection." Let's set the visual metaphor aside and listen. Isn't the fact that we are here, speaking, proof of that? An assumedly lost author speaks with her subject; the absurdity of the subject commenting on her work; the exhilaration in finding meaning in wordplay; that laughter, fundamental and excessive, against the rhetoric that demands criticism to be "sober," "robust." Apparent lightness to talk depths, a secret dimension of understanding that is not formless. The Mysteries are not owned, like a thought, not applied, like a formula. They are a csite that offers something ulterior any time you return there. But to return there you must leave it, repeatedly, go back, haunt—

C.: —and be haunted.[11] Watch out, D.C. You are beginning to write like An Authority In The Field, and I am beginning to have tremors at the thought.

D.C.: Did you know there is a brand of mixing desks called Soundcraft / Ghost? To make an audio track, craft needs ghost, ghost needs craft, not as a dualism but duality, the two at once, not one without the other.

C.: Someone else would say now, "Stop, D.C., your manners of thinking are unsettling and composite, moving from myth to literature to music language. I cannot follow you." But I cherish your chimeric contraptions, lopsided as they are.

D.C.: Don't you see how the specific—

C.: —lopsided, admit it—

D.C.: —choice of forms and materials is my critical understanding, my discernment, this, not the other? The choice is *not* to refer to certain names, and to open a csite for others. Don't you

---

11 Ibid., 439.

see, this my manner of keeping myself more speciously groundless?

C. [suddenly benevolent]: Your chimeric way of presenting and connecting certain texts makes me want to spend time with them. You give me a glimpse of your experience of reading them and prompt me to read them in turn. You take me there, instead of claiming authority over them. At the same time, you do not illustrate everything. You ask me to work with you, take initiative, look up words or concepts, at times imagine or distort them. There is something about the physical *and* poetic act of having to look up or imagine words, follow up clues from your texts, that makes the knowledge gained in this way more present and persistent. You put me through a process, not just offer me a list of conclusions. May I say it: this is criticism as we need it.

D.C.: Criticism in the choice of its subjects, criticism whose artifice is made evident; criticism of desire and doing, working with and inside the material. Criticism that makes its limitations visible, its *nothing to say* an understanding of absence rather than the absence of understanding; a scrutiny of the contexts and circumstances by which a critic apparently has no words, as she is attuned to lower signals; a prompt to consider less conventional manners, as we need it.

C.: You use we a lot, D.C. This may be problematic for some.

D.C.: We need we. My we does not signal a universal truth but momentarily holds the voices I modulate when I write. It is the intimate, chimeric *we of you and I,* of this conversation, here, now. *You who speak to me, you who narrate me,* as in the literal translation of the title of Adriana Cavarero's book, dryly translated in the English edition as *Relating Narratives*.[12]

---

12 Adriana Cavarero, *Tu che mi guardi, tu che mi racconti: Filosofia della narrazione* (Milan: Feltrinelli, 1997), and *Relating Narratives: Storytelling and Selfhood,* trans. P.A. Kottman (New York: Routledge, 2000).

C.: She is one who truly understands me, Chimera, and often allows me to appear at the end of her books.

D.C.: At the end of *Inclinations* for example, closing nearly two hundred pages of her *critique of rectitude* with a nod to the smile in Leonardo da Vinci's *The Virgin and Child with St. Anne,* "a form of altruism that presents itself as unusual, problematic, even unheard of, but all the same tangible in the detached and serene smile of Leonardo's *Madonna*," the ambiguous smile of a "secret peace" —

C.: Another secret.

D.C.: — the same secret peace of the mystics, a secret peace suggesting that "there is a carnal sense of existence, as mundane as it is prosaic —

C.: Chimeric.

D.C.: — that consists primarily in her irrevocable inclination toward the other. […] The clues to her secret, like so many Renaissance enigmas, are so obvious that they have remained altogether invisible to the preoccupied gaze of the intellect."[13]

C.: The ending of this book floored you at the time.

D.C.: How couldn't it? Consider the shift in mood, the horizon it opens by moving the attention, in those last two pages, toward a quality of the gaze so human and at once, so mysterious. It guided my thinking toward chimeric writing as a way of orientation and multiple selfhood, a we of sympathetic frequencies, a we of resonance not coercion. No wonder that Cavarero is an acute reader of Dinesen and mentions the story of Pellegrina

---

13 Adriana Cavarero, *Inclinations: A Critique of Rectitude*, trans. Amanda Minervini and Adam Sitze (Stanford: Stanford University Press, 2016), 174–75.

Leoni, again in the last two pages of *Relating Narratives*. *Pellegrinare* in Italian is to journey, and indeed Pellegrina journeys through many identities, yet her story is singular. "The uniqueness of the existent has no need of a form that plans or contains it."[14] It is one and changing, here and elsewhere, csiting "as in the dream of a fable, or perhaps, as a desire that is not exchanged for its dream."[15]

C.: A desire not exchanged for its dream. A chimera.

D.C.: Cavarero wrote of the basic human need for each to hear one's story through the voice of another, its unique call to be answered back. Laura (Riding) Jackson called it "the story of us."[16] Pasolini wrote "death is not in being unable to communicate, but in no longer being understood."[17] *We* demands —

C.: — we demand —

D.C.: — reception and attention, singular, specific.

C.: You may be wishing for a chorus of approval now but hold back. I am not entirely satisfied. We must talk more around your ideas of inhabitation and haunting. In *Petrolio*, Pasolini showed various degrees of inhabitation of his materials through kinship: from ponderous pages formed through Dostoevsky's *The Demons*, to the dialogue between two personified concepts in front of the main character's body, lifted from Lucian to that most direct inhabitation and slight variance in a name, *Petronio, Petrolio*. Petronio, the Italian for Petronius, was the author of the *Satyricon*, and *Petrolio* is the title of Pasolini's book, which he

---

14 Cavarero, *Relating Narratives*, 144.
15 Ibid.
16 Laura (Riding) Jackson, *The Telling*, ed. Michael Schmidt (Manchester: Carcanet, 2005), 43.
17 Pier Paolo Pasolini, "Una disperata vitalità / A Desperate Vitality," in *Poems*, trans. Norman McAfee (New York: Farrar, Straus & Giroux, 1996), 150–51.

considered to be a modern *Satyricon*. No explanations, glosses, or evaluations. He is in a name that is another's. Sited, cited, csited. In a name, in a small variance. What discernment in this subtle move.

D.C.: You are acute, Chim. You may begin to understand how, in my idea of writing you, critical writing does not have to go elsewhere than itself to gain evidence of its yearning for its subjects. In fact, to gain evidence is not the point, the yearning is. Dare I say it, yearning *is* the evidence.

C.: All and nothing.

D.C.: "I may feel all and feel nothing," I heard in an exquisite sonnet. Nothing: the feeling of emptiness, anxiety, inability I perceive every time I set out to write with the demands and pressure of producing a clear statement, argument, or overview. In front of Calasso's books, for example, what can I possibly say, what more, who am I, and where? I can say less, yearn chimerically for them in reading and then, by contrast, All appears; the fullness, the drive, the embodiment, the dizzying restlessness in finding a form that is not accomplished or exhaustive, but holds the metamorphoses of understanding which I go through in reading. Chimeric yearning is the space in which I can finally say something —

C.: And that finally is never final, never complete, it marks a rebeginning.

D.C.: — say something while holding desire for my subjects, my movement with, and my being moved by their words, instead of the paralysis in front of the demand for accomplished, concluded evaluations. This is what I understood in Corbin's exhortation, found in his study of Ibn 'Arabi, to become "disciples of Khidr." A complex, not entirely definable entity in Sufism, Khidr's guidance does not consist "in leading all his disciples uniformly to the same goal […], identical for all, in the manner of a theologian propagating his dogma. He leads each disciple to his own theophany," which corresponds to "the form of his own being," to his own sympathetic correspondence with the subject of his desire.[18] Knowledge is not about attaining Khidr but about learning to see the "Khidr of your being."[19] You might begin to see the consequences of this line of thinking when applied to teaching, to ways of prompting and transmitting knowledge, of forming understanding around a work, not through the filter of dogma but through that of singular encounters and conversations.

C.: All and nothing, revealing and concealing.

D.C.: How to hold you, chimera, in writing? Writing. Writing as if the commentary became the primary source; an acknowledgement of reception and transmission, a recognition that the resonances heard in study bring the asynchronous structures of reading together, their teachings received from another as in a porous reading. Finding and reinstating through presence and practice. This is why I do not want to give any prescriptions around chimeric writing but write it. So tell me now, who are you?

C.: I am this.

D.C.: You did not say, "I am." You said, "I am this." You call for me to say it too, to write *you*.

C.: Complicated and convoluted, that is, this, me. You realize what it means, to try and hold me, to circle around the impossible, the subject of a yearning, in a context in which you are

---

18 Henry Corbin, "Sophiology and Devotio Sympathetica", in *Alone with the Alone: Creative Imagination in the Sufism of Ibn 'Arabi,* trans. Ralph Manheim (Princeton: Princeton University Press, 1998), 61.
19 Ibid.

supposed to lay out aims, methods, cases, achievements, conclusions.

D.C.: That is why one day I vanished. Until then I continued to write, in formal as much as conceptual repetitions and reoccurrences always slightly out of synch. I wanted my readers to understand what it means to be a stranger in a language — to inhabit it, to be there, and always slightly *off*. In English I could not hear myself in full. Then can you begin to understand how often my language fell into the temptation of assonance, pun, or rhyme to get an illusion of presence, to spare itself the feeling of not being true. Can you imagine the void and, at once, the laughter?

C.: I am beginning to understand. Your idea of writing is such a chimera.

D.C.: You can see my embarrassment, my frustration, when they asked me to define you.

C.: Define me? How dare they?

D.C.: *Theorize*, even! It took me years, and much effort, to lay some grounds for my approach, which studies manners of orientation, tensions, and undercurrents that exist beneath words.

C.: I recall, now that you mention the way you go about your language being formed in literature, hearing faint echoes of verses of songs and poems in your earlier works, which lingered at the back of perception, never fully disclosed…

D.C.: They will never fully be, except for those who follow hints and suggestions scattered in the pages. The intention was always for my prose to sound vaguely familiar but impossible to circumscribe.

C.: *An image of Echo and Chimera —*

D.C.: — and the transmissions emitted from that image. Writing was never for closure, but an attempt to hand over some material, in the full awareness of dealing often in dead currencies.

C.: Then probably the nature and forms of the transmission become more relevant.

D.C.: I will read to you now some sketches for a treatise on illegibility, which I started to assemble before my disappearance:

"On Illegibility — By D.C., not a writer of note, but a writer of nothing." There are forms and histories of reading that offer ways of understanding as being with their materials, fleeting and complex as they may be. They can afford not to narrate, not to function as —

C.: Why a treatise? Your subject matter lacks a single purpose. I beg you, D.C., enough with this pathetic completist *élan*. Speak with me. I am your subject, I matter. You may be disappointed at not being perceived as an accomplished writer, but at least you will have *one* interlocutor who listens. Tell me now, in your own words, from whomever they may have been taken — no, what was the expression Robert Duncan used? — *derived,* tell me about the illegibility in this form of criticism that takes my name and does not want to be held together by narrative or conclusive arcs.[20]

D.C.: I am keen to specify it is not only my words to be derived from others. My silences are too.

C.: Aren't you meticulous.

---

20 "As, in writing, deriving as I do, I burn the nets of my origins." Robert Duncan, *The H.D. Book,* eds. Michael Boughn and Victor Coleman (Berkeley: University of California Press, 2011), 219.

D.C.: Meticulous, specious, inflexible. One of my concerns, in the sketch for the treatise that you have so unceremoniously interrupted, was to read with my ears, across the density of references across languages. To read with one's ears is an inversion typical of mystic discourse, which signals depth and pres — Chim, are you awake?

[Chimera snores loudly.]

D.C. [in a preachy monologic fit, rushing her words before the composite monster wakes up]: Charles Bernstein has denounced the implied principles for peer-reviewed journals which suggest "preference for a lifeless prose, bloated with the compulsory repetitive explanation of what every other 'important' piece on this subject has said. Of course, many professors will insist that they do not subscribe to this, but the point is not what any one of us does, but the institutional culture we accept."[21] A tacit agreement, for which to write in an informed, reflexive, research-based and critical manner, implies compliance with given standards of tone, and form so that everyone can operate on a levelled plane, and "be understood." We get to that paradoxical point, he continues, where "a wide range of ideas" are published, *as long as they are expressed in the dominant style.*[22] As if the actual tone and form of writing did not count. "From an educational point of view, it might be better to insist that what is inaccessible or impossible to grasp is exactly what needs to be taught in our schools."[23] I could not agree more. I still recall how I could guide my most reluctant art students to write their dissertations, during my teaching days on Earth. It had to do with attempting to find forms and arrangements that would chimerically transform the materials and movements of their artistic practices into text. We worked toward understand-

---

21 Charles Bernstein, "A Blow Is Like an Instrument: The Poetic Imaginary and Curricular Practices," in *Attack of the Difficult Poems: Essays and Inventions* (Chicago: The University of Chicago Press, 2011), 16.
22 Ibid.
23 Ibid., 20.

ing that writing critically about their practices did not demand sites of clarity, but csites of attention and complexity; not explanations, but transformations, and conversations. We challenged ourselves to stop quoting from writers and theorists given as external frameworks of legitimization, authority, and recognition (those we felt we *had* to refer to but that did not *feel* in the same way as the texture of our work) and to think instead of texts that were necessary, not imposed, to our understanding of the context and reach of what we did. The exercise was to challenge those names dropped during a studio visit, "it makes me think of…," and think of something else instead; to develop ways of scrutiny into the manners in which thinking forms, not by obligation, but by necessity. One sentence, lived through, one page, fully pondered, one book, read with attention rather than the usual serviceable quotes. The question was, *how did we encounter the writers we are quoting?* Are they meaningful to our reasoning, are we mentioning them because they are easier to access? Is there anyone else who may contribute deeper to our understanding? Are we silencing someone else just because to present them would require more work? Beware of attaching formulas to the practice just because they are easy to recognize, therefore guarantee visibility. Do not think of *framing*—the verb "to frame" reduces it to a two-dimensional, enclosed entity. Allow your thought to move, allow its core to manifest itself from its workings, and all it corresponds to and with. It is the intensity of a relationship with references as living heartbeats that matters here. To find language working against language, holding exactly that excess of an artistic practice and at once, finding ways for it through words; that ungraspable quality can never be kept yet informs writing. It is a speculative gesture and, as such, deeply significant for artists: could students start to write thinking of rhythms, textures, amplitudes, signals? What form of writing takes shape, that is necessarily tied to a way of being with material, not arbitrary? This book could have been something else, it would have been written as *a monograph*—

[Chimera jolts in her sleep, disturbed at her subliminal, certainly not sublime, proximity with the term "monograph," as she recalls that thundering dictum by one Ansgar Allen around monographs "being the graveyard of the intellect."][24]

D.C.: — then it would have perpetuated existing approaches to the writing of research. As long as it is formed the way it is formed, and exactly because of its form, it opens up to a manner and a model of writing which does, and is, something else. In turn, it teaches and practices other forms of reading, and of listening. If I could go back to Earth and continue to teach, I would design a course around form and excess of speech in mystic discourse: Teresa of Ávila, stating that we are where we are and the most difficult thing is to enter; Angelus Silesius rhyming *schrift* and *nicht,* writing and nothing;[25] Jean-Joseph Surin and his understanding of discourse that "forms desire, desire bound to nothing,"[26] *The Cloud of Unknowing* staging the eloquent, elusive, ceaseless tension between writing and silence, presence and self-effacement, gesturing toward chimeras.

C. [wakes up, on hearing her name]: Did you call me?

D.C.: I did not think you were so sensitive to such superficial flattery as a simple mention of your name. Listen, I know you were bored, but this is not to be missed. I must say something about not understanding but standing inside, being present.

C.: As long as you do not overwhelm my hearing with your wordy sententious meanderings. I am getting tired of our logomachy.

---

24 Ansgar Allen, *The Sick List* (Norwich: Boiler House Press, 2021), 5.
25 Michel de Certeau, *The Mystic Fable: The Sixteenth and Seventeeth Centuries,* Vol. 2, trans. Michael B. Smith (Chicago: University of Chicago Press, 2015), 137.
26 Michel de Certeau, *The Mystic Fable: The Sixteenth and Seventeeth Centuries,* Vol. 1, trans. Michael B. Smith (Chicago: University of Chicago Press, 1992), 167.

D.C.: I want to tell you of a specific case of being out of sync. You have known me for a long time, Chim, long before I disappeared. You will remember how I was brought up in Italy, in the late 1970s and '80s, in a state school system in which we learned Latin like we learned History or Maths. In Italian, Latin is integral to language. Some Latin terms or expressions are parts of it and are used in a manner that is not exceptional, exclusive, or pertaining to jargon. We use them without thinking about it, it is not a contrived effort to display a privileged education. Imagine when, on using Latin in English, I found myself labelled as elitist.

C.: Ah, the "awful nightmare of sameness."[27]

D.C.: To avoid using Latin in English would mean censoring parts of language that are living elements of how I think and perceive. It would be like asking me to stop gesticulating when I speak in English. I will not. I cannot entrench myself in my position either. I can say more about how my understanding forms through language according to a different system, and perhaps, not less importantly, ask readers to pay attention, listen to another manner of being in language which is not immediate, before going straight to the *judge and exclude* response, as Bernstein said, to "respond to the process of discovery."[28]

C.: I want to move on from the presumed illegibility in your use of Latin, to the thickness of a prose densely woven with unusual references, another form of illegibility which I sometimes heard brought up in some superficial remarks around David Toop's books. "Too many references," they would remark, "they go over my head." Over a bridge, I would throw them.

---

27 Charles Bernstein, *A Poetics* (Cambridge: Harvard University Press, 1998), 175.
28 Ibid.

D.C.: Lazy, how lazy can readers be, how willing to blandly give their trust and time only to reassuring, familiar references. But I am in search of a certain dissonance, of more troubled writing. That trouble was exactly why I was drawn to *difficult* books, as I read them not for recognition but for a sense of attraction and discovery, ignited by them. I recall my first encounters with *Ocean of Sound,* even more with *Exotica,* as if I was given the keys to a parallel world of music I had never heard before, but the manner in which those materials were arranged made the difference.[29] Reading I was enchanted, under a spell, not instructed. Unlike comprehensive, systematic treatises that by explaining and contextualizing music unknown to me in a fortress of perfection left me feeling inadequate and excluded, *Exotica* was composite and fragmentary, a porous fabric of perception in which I could add my own, flawed and naive as I may have been. The sounds Toop wrote about were interwoven with memories and personal experiences, they appeared as possibilities rather than prescribed and described items. Those pages offered a matrix of perception, not rules. They made me want to hear those sounds before I heard them. They took me outside themselves, in my singular pursuits which in turn led met to more discoveries. They took me deeper into the working of a mind-with-words into the pages, into what writing could do with and inside its subject matters, not against their grain.

C.: "I had to create my own sense, my own soul even, out of remote exotic zones that came and went of their own unpredictable volition,"[30] Toop writes. I was there, in the blissful unexplainable synchronization of three people in a car, the Dutch landscape, and the music of Jeff Mills, "flooded with panic and exhilaration, the shock of outrunning time."[31] You did not even

---

29 David Toop, *Exotica: Fabricated Soundscapes in a Real World* (London: Serpent's Tail, 1999), and *Ocean of Sound: Aether Talk, Ambient Sound and Imaginary Worlds* (London: Serpent's Tail, 1995).
30 Toop, *Exotica*, xiv.
31 Ibid., 14–16.

know who Jeff Mills was when you read this, yet it affected you profoundly.

D.C.: Not being a specialist in the subject matter of that book heightened my perception of its form. That cannot be overlooked: how those words moved, how they were assembled, moving along the changing RPMs of the music.

C.: How chimeric. Have I heard this before?

D.C.: Perhaps you heard of "the condition of music." It is a phrase I found in a February 6, 1923 journal entry by Mary Butts, writer of liminal states into life, into landscaped forms of being, into short stories and novels that feature psyche, mood, atmosphere as significantly as their characters, and into journals and essays as affected by the unsayable as her fiction. In the journal she lists a number of encounters during her day, including "the Museum & the King who has the face of my daimon," and concludes, "all these were part of one thing, the condition of music. This was not easy to write down."[32] A couple of years later, in October 1925, she mentions "something that one is always at the point of being about to say. A form that has the shape of a content which is a new arrangement."[33]

C.: This was not easy to write down.

D.C.: I wish to dwell on the state which leads a writer to remark, "this was not easy to write down." To linger on what is apprehended and diffused, if I think of *the condition of music* as a chimeric state that allows speechlessness to prompt more words rather than inhibit them, words that are *volume*: resonant space, signal, text. It is akin to Lispector's silence rising "subtly from

---

32 Mary Butts, *The Journals of Mary Butts,* ed. Nathalie Blondel (New Haven: Yale University Press, 2002), 202.
33 Ibid., 217.

the knock of the phrases,"[34] to the hum of Calasso's mad impurities, to the song of my *sirena*-chimera that I heard in Stampa through Campo. You must understand, I never set up chimeric writing as a new, groundbreaking theory. Aware of what is around, it manifests a way of arranging words and thoughts, and moving in them. It cannot be simply put as theory, as it would lose much of its density and impetus if set aside from the present-absent substance which is allowing you and I to speak. Chimeric writing slips away, is formed in subtle variance and the way it lingers, like the impression left by the telling of a story, by the playing of a record. It is, in words, in the way they are chosen, assembled, treated. And the question is not, what can I say? but, how can I arrange, and transmit what I hear, as it is connected in my understanding?

C.: Making research an issue of new arrangements, of how we move our words and transmit them.

D.C.: Not research as in *I came first, discovered, own* but as *I tune in*; not concerned with unearthing treasures, or with exclusivity. It does not dismiss, in its form, the initial confusion of being in an unfamiliar space. Then, I want to faint.

C.: Fainting, that old literary trick of ellipsis and imagination for characters, for narrative, and for you. You have been using it eminently, and I hear echoes of Dante, who at the end of *Inferno*'s Fifth Canto in the *Divine Comedy* (another D.C.) faints, overwhelmed with emotion at the story of the two lovers Paolo and Francesca, full of sighs and tears, a story told as someone who cries and speaks at once, exhausted by the yearning.[35] Then I recall that most languid story of 'Ali ibn Bakkar and Shams al-Nahar in the *Arabian Nights,* extreme and exhausted tale of

---

34 Clarice Lispector, *Áqua viva,* trans. Stefan Tobler (London: Penguin Books, 2014), 15.
35 Dante Alighieri, "Inferno: Canto V," in *La Divina Commedia* (Milan-Padova: Euroricerca, 1977), 41.

being sick into love, in which two characters who will never be together continue to faint, night after night, and the more they do, the more exhilarating the sense of longing and yearning becomes.³⁶

D.C.: Fainting as a recurring psychic space of exhaustion and disorientation, the oscillatory presence in which we exist with our materials, rather than a literal interpretation or presentation of evidence. Everything is undocumented, yet it is there, chimerically. Signifying, and disturbed.

C.: It flees… And it is almost time for you to sleep again. What is it you wish to tell me before you return to silence?

D.C.: A passing thought.

C.: I am used by now to your woefully inconclusive remarks.

D.C.: When Blanchot writes of the neuter, I think he wants to listen, although he does not explicitly say so. "[T]he narrative voice neither reveals nor conceals."³⁷ This does not mean it signifies nothing, and "it does not signify in the same way the invisible-visible signifies […] [and] it opens another power in the language, one alien to the power of illumination."³⁸ The light/shade, transparency/opacity is "an inveterate metaphor," and he wants to find a different way. Listening to the subtle noise of prose, I think. "[T]he narrative voice is the most critical one that can communicate unheard. That is why we tend, as we listen to it, to confuse it with the oblique voice of unhappiness or the oblique voice of madness."³⁹ He speaks of voice, he wants to

---

36 Malcom C. Lyons, trans., *The Arabian Nights: Tales of 1001 Nights* (London: Penguin Classics, 2010), 2:650–92.
37 Maurice Blanchot, "The Narrative Voice (the 'he,' the neuter)," in *The Gaze of Orpheus and Other Literary Essays,* ed. P. Adams Sitney, trans. Lydia Davis (New York: Station Hill, 1981), 142.
38 Ibid.
39 Ibid., 143.

listen. Isn't the *kind of void in the work* my chimeric vessel, the space of reverberation that hosts the humming beyond words, that words momentarily host?

C.: Such a cluttered and confusing argument, D.C., you, always momentarily, always else, always away, always yearning. Go back to your timeless sleep, now.

[D.C. faints.]

VfaF: So the story of these words goes; a voice, a song, a csite, a loss, a chord.

Imaginary Conversation

Cristina Rovina and Chimera

Cristina Rovina: I need your enquiring mind today, Chim. I need your fire to probe the unsayable. I spent this morning thinking.

Chimera: Did you say *singing*?

C.R.: If my song is that "song which is no song at all," heard at the end of Cage's *Lecture on Nothing,* then yes, Chim, I spent the morning singing.[1] Remember, Teresa of Ávila would often open a book because it *kept a place,* D.C. says.[2] It allowed her to listen, to become volume, to sing her song which is no song at all. When you sing, you are where you are and you are other.

C.: You csite.

C.R.: These are the news I have for you here. It is necessary to stop and mark the difficulty, the friction that some subjects, some chimeras provoke, rather than assuming it is all fine, and

---
1 John Cage, "Lecture on Nothing," in *Silence: Lectures and Writings* (New York: Marion Boyars, 2009), 126.
2 Michel de Certeau, "Absolute Reading", in *The Mystic Fable: The Sixteenth and Seventeeth Centuries,* Vol. 2, trans. Michael B. Smith (Chicago: The University of Chicago Press, 2015), 127.

words will manage somehow. It is necessary to stop and mark these difficult moments. Sometimes words are found while stating the difficulty to write rather than ignoring it. To do so, I need to find ways of arranging words, to articulate what falls in the gaps of conventional syntax or lexicon, like Harry Partch did when he built new musical instruments and called for other manners of tuning them so that they would expand the range of what could be sounded, heard. He never placed emphasis on polish. He called instead for *extraverbal magic*,[3] capable to inject new life into the otherwise "pathetically impoverished language of tone."[4] Consider the time spent working through such invisible material. The *volume* of words is as much criticism as it is argument, it carries the argument as it is formed.

C. [chiming]: I am chimeric.

C.R.: Words are a *not yet,* a yearning which brings D.C. back into being, in my words, knowing she is here, and never entirely hearn.

C.: An effective rhetorical device in itself.

C.R.: Call it device, or D.'s vice, certainly a necessary one.

C.: Are you inviting me?

C.R.: I am inviting you to sing a cover song with me, two heartbeats at once, one voice, the other, yearning. Musicians speak of *putting your spin* into a cover song, of *owning it,* showing at once no respect, and total respect. You desire the song, you sing, but the words are not yours.

---

[3] Harry Partch, "A Soul Tormented by Contemporary Music Looks for a Humanizing Alchemy: 'The Bewitched,'" in *Bitter Music: Collected Journals, Essays, Introductions, and Librettos* (Champaign: University of Illinois Press, 1991), 239.
[4] Ibid., 161.

C.: You think, but the words are not yours.

C.R.: Are they? No pressure to be faithful. This comes from pleasure, not pressure.

C.: When you sing a cover song you may catch yourself unguarded, other.

C.R.: The pure fruits go crazy.

A Cover Song of Chimeras

The voices of Chimera, D.C., C.R., from a Faintspeaker, at times overlapping, at times interfering, as composite one, never as tutti: So the story goes, actually it does not go anywhere, it stays, very close to the writer who used to go in and out of sanatoriums, roaratoriums, and songs.[1] She'd been living like that for some time, going farther and farther in her migrations, and the definitive gesture was to split the analysis from the embodiment, in other words, to hear, to stay, to here, to csite. Writing could not be sustained otherwise. It had to be a ruin, incomplete material. Sometimes it was enough to consider that which was not there, to place the descriptions, the facts, aside, allow the rest to roar undisturbed, like the impressions left by the telling of a story, by the playing of a record, or conversations, even imagined ones, imagined but no less real. — — — She had long known that to know is to suffer an emotion and to be in a certain state. She began a fugue into becoming many voices. She knew she had to suffer their commotion, and similarly words must be formed, as commotions, where echoes abandon themselves to inertia,

---

[1] This section is in part a mix and distortion of Roberto Calasso as he echoes, distorts, and mixes Gottfried Benn in "Cicatrice di smalto," *in I quarantanove gradini* (Milan: Adelphi, 1991), 475–86. Its echo was first heard in Daniela Cascella, "Untitled," in *Dominique Hurth: Mixtape*, cassette and booklet, artist edition, Berlin, 2020.

rhythms wink at one another, nouns, like frequencies, merge, or beat, and she, and the other she, and the other, all of them, no longer see what they are writing but continue to hear and rearrange signals; the irruption of a crepuscular state as a condition of consciousness. — — — This is not about style but a question of substance. Voices grow like creepers between the heavy grey paving stones of thought. Strangely familiar and estranging even for ears accustomed to extreme meanderings. It was said that those who like strophes also like catastrophes, those who like statues also need to stand for ruins. Their voices are not always polished, at times they are many-layered, overloaded, at times a hint of underlying melody does not come through entirely, or it does so in excess, at times it remains imprisoned in the thickly-woven meshes of experiment. Does it matter? A specific attunement can be sensed, a cadence that exceeds formal constraints. There will be time later for order. First the catastrophe, then the strophes. Later, when the excess of sound reenters the structure, it confuses categories even more. How can these voices be at once radiance and structure? How to obey the fluctuations of movement and at once set up a rule of form? It is tolerable to follow one of those avenues, but both? Yet, if you don't follow both you lose them, and the sounds elude you: to hear them, to hear them, you need to hear, radiance in structure, structure in radiance. Bounded and immeasurable, an echo, of the same substance of these walls. Where to find, in these walls, the longing which gives echo its purpose, its boundless spaces? What remains in stillness, or in the slow circling? A residue, even if it was only dust, even if it was corners, even if the signal was faint. Linger on, where you heard the voices committed to you. The place of their frequencies is on the periphery, their area is mutation, never mute, not univocal. — — — Remember again, the csite. I still have the name, not the coordinates. I was nearly there, but not quite, have always been there, and have never been. Damp air of moldering land, abandoned hothouses, roses. Could they host that one who is impure and composite? Then perhaps it might be said, "I threw my self at all the winds of heaven, but kept my attention to echoes. It is little—it is all, it is nothing—it is life itself."[2] A presence, sounding, stringing, probing; to become, a voice inside would scream, salt and fire in the eyes, what else can anyone carry, anyone who hears this? Use your means, know your ways, you must have hearn and held much to no longer be anything but a voice, a song, a csite, a loss, a chord, a chime, chimera.

---

[2] An echo and distortion of Roberto Calasso, *The Ruin of Kasch*, trans. Richard Dixon (London: Penguin Books, 2018), 339.

Bibliography

Alighieri, Andrea di Serego, and Nicola Masciandaro, eds. *Glossator Journal* 11: "Cristina Campo: Translation / Commentary" (2021).
Alighieri, Dante. "Inferno: Canto V." In *La Divina Commedia*, 33–41. Milan-Padova: Euroricerca, 1977.
Allen, Ansgar. *The Sick List*. Norwich: Boiler House Press, 2021.
Apuleius. *The Golden Ass*. Translated by P.G. Walsh. Oxford: Oxford University Press, 2008.
Bachelard, Gaston. *Lautréamont*. Translated by Robert S. Dupree. Dallas: The Pegasus Foundation, 1986.
Bachmann, Ingeborg. *Letteratura come utopia*. Translated by Vanda Perretta. Milan: Adelphi, 1993.
Bakhtin, Mikhail. *Problems of Dostoevsky's Poetics*. Edited and translated by Caryl Emerson. Minneapolis: University of Minnesota Press, 1984.
Baudelaire, Charles. "Chacun sa chimère." In *Piccoli poemi in prosa,* translated by Nicola Muschitiello, 84–87. Milan: Rizzoli, 1990.
Benn, Gottfried. *Lo smalto sul nulla*. Translated by Luciano Zagari, Giancarlo Russo, and Gilberto Forti. Milan: Adelphi, 1992.
Bernstein, Charles. *A Poetics*. Cambridge: Harvard University Press, 1998.

———. *Attack of the Difficult Poems: Essays and Inventions.* Chicago: The University of Chicago Press, 2011.

Blanchfield, Brian. *Proxies: Essays Near Knowing.* New York: Nightboat Books, 2016.

Blanchot, Maurice. *Lautréamont and Sade.* Translated by Stuart Kendall and Michelle Kendall. Stanford: Stanford University Press, 2004.

———. *The Gaze of Orpheus and Other Literary Essays.* Edited by P. Adams Sitney. Translated by Lydia Davis. New York: Station Hill, 1981.

———. *The Infinite Conversation.* Translated by Susan Hanson. Minneapolis: University of Minnesota Press, 2016.

Bojesen, Emile. "Conversation as Educational Research." *Educational Philosophy and Theory* 51, no. 6 (2019): 650–59. DOI: 10.1080/00131857.2018.1508995.

Borges, Jorge Luis. "The False Problem of Ugolino." In *Selected Non-Fictions,* edited by Eliot Weinberger, translated by Esther Allen, Suzanne Jill Levine, and Eliot Weinberger, 278–79. London: Penguin Books, 1999.

Boyer, Anne. *A Handbook of Disappointed Fate.* New York: Ugly Duckling Presse, 2018.

Briggs, Kate. *This Little Art.* London: Fitzcarraldo Editions, 2017.

Browne, Sir Thomas. *Religio Medici and Hydriotaphia, or Urne-Buriall.* Edited by Stephen Greenblatt and Ramie Targoff. New York: New York Review of Books, 2012.

Butts, Mary. *The Journals of Mary Butts.* Edited by Nathalie Blondel. New Haven: Yale University Press, 2002.

Cage, John. "Lecture on Nothing." In *Silence: Lectures and Writings,* 109–26. New York: Marion Boyars, 2009.

Calasso, Roberto. *I quarantanove gradini.* Milan: Adelphi, 1991.

———. *Il cacciatore celeste.* Milan: Adelphi, 2019.

———. *L'ardore.* Milan: Adelphi, 2016.

———. *L'impuro folle.* Milan: Adelphi, 1992.

———. *Literature and the Gods.* Translated by Tim Parks. London: Vintage, 2001.

———. *The Ruin of Kasch*. Translated by Richard Dixon. London: Penguin Books, 2018.
Campana, Dino. "La Chimera." In *Canti Orfici*, 105–6. Milan: Rizzoli, 1989.
Campo, Cristina. *Gli imperdonabili*. Milan: Adelphi, 1987.
———. *Il mio pensiero non vi lascia*. Milan: Adelphi, 2011.
Cascella, Daniela. *En Abîme: Listening, Reading, Writing: An Archival Fiction*. Winchester: Zero Books, 2012.
———. *F.M.R.L.: Footnotes, Mirages, Refrains and Leftovers of Writing Sound*. Winchester: Zero Books, 2015.
———. *Singed: Muted Voice-Transmissions, After the Fire*. Prague and London: Equus Press, 2017.
———. "The Secret Euphoria of Reading: On 'Cento lettere a uno sconosciuto' by Roberto Calasso." *3:AM Magazine*, November 24, 2015. https://www.3ammagazine.com/3am/the-secret-euphoria-of-reading-on-cento-lettere-a-uno-sconosciuto-by-roberto-calasso/.
———. "The Stain of Stein: For Chimeric Writing." *Tinted Window* 2: "Verbivocovisual" (November 2019).
———. "Untitled." In *Dominique Hurth: Mixtape*. Cassette and booklet, artist edition. Berlin, 2020.
Cavarero, Adriana. *Inclinations: A Critique of Rectitude*. Translated by Amanda Minervini and Adam Sitze. Stanford: Stanford University Press, 2016.
———. *Relating Narratives: Storytelling and Selfhood*. Translated by P.A. Kottman. New York: Routledge, 2000.
———. *Tu che mi guardi, tu che mi racconti: Filosofia della narrazione*. Milan: Feltrinelli, 1997.
Cheetham, Tom. *The World Turned Inside Out: Henry Corbin and Islamic Mysticism*. New Orleans: Spring Journal Books, 2015.
Cixous, Hélène. "The Laugh of the Medusa." Translated by Keith Cohen and Paula Cohen. *Signs* 1, no. 4 (Summer 1976): 875–93. https://www.jstor.org/stable/3173239.
———. *Three Steps on the Ladder of Writing*. Translated by Sarah Cornell and Susan Sellers. New York: Columbia University Press, 1993.

Clifford, James. "The Pure Products Go Crazy." In *The Predicament of Culture: Twentieth-Century Ethnography, Literature, and Art*, 1–17. Cambridge: Harvard University Press, 1988.
Corbin, Henry. *Alone with the Alone: Creative Imagination in the Sufism of Ibn 'Arabi*. Translated by Ralph Manheim. Princeton: Princeton University Press, 1998.
———. *Avicenna and the Visionary Recital*. Translated by Willard R. Trask. Princeton: Princeton University Press, 1988.
Darroch-Lozowski, Vivian. *Voice of Hearing*. Toronto: Squint Press, 2020.
de Boron, Robert. "La visione." Translated by Cristina Campo. In *I mistici dell'Occidente*, Vol. 1, edited by Elémire Zolla, 769–70. Milan: Adelphi, 2010.
de Certeau, Michel. *The Mystic Fable: The Sixteenth and Seventeeth Centuries*. Vol. 1. Translated by Michael B. Smith. Chicago: The University of Chicago Press, 1992.
———. *The Mystic Fable: The Sixteenth and Seventeeth Centuries*. Vol. 2. Translated by Michael B. Smith. Chicago: The University of Chicago Press, 2015.
de Nerval, Gérard. "The Chimeras: Golden Lines." Translated by Robert Duncan. In *Aurelia and Other Writings*, translated by Geoffrey Wagner, Robert Duncan, and Marc Lowenthal, 141–65. Boston: Exact Change, 1996.
De Stefano, Cristina. *Belinda e il mostro: Vita segreta di Cristina Campo*. Milan: Adelphi, 2002.
Dinesen, Isak (Karen Blixen). "The Dreamers." In *Seven Gothic Tales*, 236–309. London: Penguin Books, 2002.
Duncan, Robert. *The H.D. Book*. Edited by Michael Boughn and Victor Coleman. Berkeley: University of California Press, 2011.
Dworkin, Craig. "The Onomastic Imagination." In *Radium of the Word: A Poetics of Materiality*, 48–78. Chicago: The University of Chicago Press, 2020.
Farnetti, Monica, and Giovanna Fozzer, eds. *Per Cristina Campo*. Milan: All'insegna del pesce d'oro, 1998.
Foscolo, Ugo. *L'ipercalisse*. 1816.

———. *Notizia intorno a Didimo Chierico.* 1813.

Frye, Northrop. *Anatomy of Criticism.* Princeton: Princeton University Press, 2020.

Fusco, Maria. "11 Statements around Art Writing." *Frieze,* October 11, 2011. https://frieze.com/article/11-statements-around-art-writing.

Griffiths, Eric. *The Printed Voice of Victorian Poetry.* Oxford: Oxford University Press, 1989.

Hearn, Lafcadio. "The Sympathy of Benten." In *Japanese Ghost Stories,* 79–85. London: Penguin Classics, 2019.

Heller-Roazen, Daniel. *Echolalias: On the Forgetting of Language.* New York: Zone Books, 2005.

Hillman, James. *Alchemical Psychology.* Putnam: Spring Publications, 2014.

Jackson, Laura (Riding). *The Telling.* Edited by Michael Schmidt. Manchester: Carcanet, 2005.

Jankélévitch, Vladimir. *Music and the Ineffable.* Translated by Carolyn Abbate. Princeton: Princeton University Press, 2003.

Jelinek, Elfriede. *Her Not All Her: On/With Robert Walser.* Translated by Damion Searls. London: Sylph Editions, 2012.

———. "Sidelined." Nobel Lecture, Swedish Academy, Stockholm, Sweden, December 7, 2004. https://www.nobelprize.org/prizes/literature/2004/jelinek/lecture/.

Jokerfull. "Carmelo Bene – La Chimera (Dino Campana)." *YouTube,* December 1, 2008. https://www.youtube.com/watch?v=6DvlyfgLDZs.

Joy, Eileen A. "Weird Reading." *Speculations: A Journal of Speculative Realism* 4 (2013): 28–34.

Julius, Rolf. *Small Music (Grau).* Edited by Bernd Schulz and Hans Gercke. Heidelberg: Kehrer Verlag, 1995.

Leopardi, Giacomo. *Operette morali.* Milan: Feltrinelli, 1998.

———. *Zibaldone di pensieri.* Milan: Feltrinelli, 2019.

Lispector, Clarice. *Água Viva.* Translated by Stefan Tobler. London: Penguin Books, 2014.

Lucian of Samosata. "The Vision: A Chapter of Autobiography." In *The Works of Lucian of Samosata,* translated by

H.W. Fowler and F.G. Fowler, 20–23. Charleston: Forgotten Books, 2007.

Manganelli, Giorgio. *Le interviste impossibili.* Milan: Adelphi, 1997.

———. "Ma Kafka non esiste." In *Il rumore sottile della prosa,* 118–21. Milan: Adelphi, 1994.

Marcus, Greil. *Lipstick Traces: A Secret History of the Twentieth Century.* Cambridge: Harvard University Press, 1989.

Masciandaro, Nicola. "Becoming Spice: Commentary as Geophilosophy." In *Collapse: Philosophical Research and Development, Volume VI: Philosophical Research and Development,* edited by Robin Mackay, 20–56. Falmouth: Urbanomic, 2010.

McGann, Jerome. *Swinburne: An Experiment in Criticism.* Chicago: University of Chicago Press, 1972.

Michaux, Henri. "Fate: B." In *A Certain Plume,* translated by Richard Sieburth, 131. New York: New York Review of Books, 2017.

O'Connor, Flannery. *Mystery and Manners: Occasional Writings.* New York: Farrar, Straus & Giroux, 1970.

Partch, Harry. *Bitter Music: Collected Journals, Essays, Introductions, and Librettos.* Champaign: University of Illinois Press, 1991.

Pasolini, Pier Paolo, dir. "La ricotta." On *Ro.Go.Pa.G* (1962/63). Eureka Entertainment, 2012. DVD.

———. "Note 3: Introduction of the Metaphysical Theme." In *Petrolio,* translated by Ann Goldstein, 6–9. London: Secker and Warburg, 1997.

———. "Una disperata vitalità / A Desperate Vitality." In *Poems,* translated by Norman McAfee, 148–77. New York: Farrar, Straus & Giroux, 1996.

Pizarnik, Alejandra. *Diarios.* Barcelona: Lumen / Penguin Random House, 2013.

———. *Extracting the Stone of Madness: Poems 1962–1972.* Translated by Yvette Siegert. New York: New Directions, 2016.

Poe, Edgar Allan. *The Complete Tales and Poems of Edgar Allan Poe*. London: Penguin Books, 1982.
Robertson, Lisa. *Nilling*. Toronto: Book*hug, 2007.
Rogoff, Irit. "'Smuggling' – An Embodied Criticality." 2006.
———."What Is a Theorist." *Transformazium Log*, May 23, 2011. http://transformazium.org/log/2011/05/irit-rogoff-what-is-a-theorist/.
Rosselli, Amelia. *La libellula*. Milan: SE, 1985.
Schreber, Daniel Paul. *Memorie di un malato di nervi*. Translated by Federico Scardanelli. Milan: Adelphi, 1974.
Spearing, A.C., trans. *The Cloud of Unknowing and Other Works*. London: Penguin Books, 2001.
Stampa, Gaspara. "Sonetto CXXIV." In *Rime* (1554).
Stein, Gertrude. *The Making of Americans*. Champaign: Dalkey Archive Press, 1995.
Steiner, George. *On Difficulty and Other Essays*. Oxford: Oxford University Press, 1978.
Stiegler, Bernard. "How I Became a Philosopher." In *Acting Out*, translated by David Barison, Daniel Ross, and Patrick Crogan Stanford, 1–35. Stanford: Stanford University Press, 2009.
Lyons, Malcom C., trans. *The Arabian Nights: Tales of 1001 Nights, Volume II*. London: Penguin Classics, 2010.
Thurman, Judith. *Isak Dinesen: The Life of Karen Blixen*. London: Penguin Books 1986.
Toop, David. *Exotica: Fabricated Soundscapes in a Real World*. London: Serpent's Tail, 1999.
———. "Gone to Earth." *David Toop: A Sinister Resonance*, September 29, 2017. https://davidtoopblog.com/2017/09/29/gone-to-earth/.
———. *Ocean of Sound: Aether Talk, Ambient Sound and Imaginary Worlds*. London: Serpent's Tail, 1995.
von Magdeburg, Mechthild. "Rivelazioni." Translated by Antonio Ballardini. In *I mistici dell'Occidente, Vol. 2*, edited by Elémire Zolla, 774–79. Milan: Adelphi, 2010.
Weil, Simone. *First and Last Notebooks*. Translated by Richard Rees. Eugene: Wipf & Stock, 2015.

———. *Gravity and Grace.* Translated by Emma Crawford and Mario von der Ruhr. New York: Routledge, 2002.

Weinberger, Eliot. *An Elemental Thing.* New York: New Directions, 2007.

Weiss, Allen S. *Breathless: Sound Recording, Disembodiment, and the Transformation of Lyrical Nostalgia.* Middletown: Wesleyan University Press, 2002.

www.ingramcontent.com/pod-product-compliance
Lightning Source LLC
Chambersburg PA
CBHW071700170426
43195CB00039B/2421